"This is a fascinating and thought-provoking e⋯⋯⋯e and hybrid worship practices. It introduces us to a rich conceptual landscape for reflecting on questions of community and participation and provides useful tools for thinking about the future shape of digitally mediated worship."
Mark Porter, research associate of religious studies at the University of Erfurt in Germany

"At a moment in which we look back and seek to assess and understand the impact of the Covid-19 pandemic on how congregations worship, Dr. Huerter's book provides a critical framework for that assessment. His research systematizes and helps provide language for a conversation that is scholarly and practical. In that sense, it is a gift to teachers in the classroom and worship leaders in churches and a welcome addition to a crucial conversation in worship and church music studies."
Marcell Silva Steuernagel, assistant professor of church music, director of the master of sacred music, and doctor of pastoral music programs at the Southern Methodist University Perkins School of Theology

"Dr. Huerter awakens us in a new day that has already dawned but has yet to reach its noontide. Whether we fear the hybrid congregation or fantasize about it, Huerter keeps our feet on the ground. He calms the fears of virtual-hesitant individuals and asks the virtual veterans to see beyond the screen. The questions raised offer an opportunity for us to reexamine our worship practices and to consider what expressions of embodiment they privilege or marginalize. This is the new book for classrooms and for church staff group study."
Terry W. York, author of *Let Our Words Become Flesh* and *Kurt Kaiser: Icon and Conscience of Contemporary Christian Music*

"With the diagnostic rigor of his academic mind and the compassionate bedside manner of his pastoral heart, Michael Huerter gives a compelling and thorough assessment of the congregation in the digital age. Especially after the mediatized dislocations of the past decade, this book lays bare the myriad interlocking systems that produced our current moment of fracture and encourages us to refocus on the task of building richly textured Christian communities, whether online or off."
Joshua Kalin Busman, assistant dean of the Esther G. Maynor Honors College and associate professor of music at University of North Carolina at Pembroke

"In *The Hybrid Congregation*, Michael Huerter does academic acrobatics to expose a critical gap between the theology and practice of online ministry and the theology and practice of church music. While attending this gap is necessary, perhaps more important is Huerter's ability to move beyond academic analyses in order to provide pastoral questions and touchstones that church leaders will do well to attend to as they navigate the issues this text raises in real time. This book is a must-read for anyone regularly navigating the opportunities and complexities of hybrid worship ministry."
Eric L. Mathis, associate pastor of The First Baptist Church of the City of Washington, DC

"Theologian and pastoral musician Michael Huerter has given us a resource to navigate the tectonic technological shift facing the church as a result of the Covid-19 pandemic. With pastoral insight, historical grounding, and theologically astute observation, Huerter guides us to redefine and reposition the effects of technological shifts on the music of the locally gathered community in the here and now. With thoughtful questions and engaging perspectives, he moves this conversation forward in ways that are clear and precise, grounded in best practice, and always rooted in an abiding love for the church and its worship. Michael Huerter has given the church a gift that comes at just the right time to triage the technological emergency to which all churches were forced to respond."

Randall Bradley, Ben H. Williams Professor of Music and director of the church music program at the Dunn Center for Christian Music Studies at Baylor University

The Hybrid Congregation

A Practical Theology of Worship
for an Online Era

Michael Huerter

An imprint of InterVarsity Press
Downers Grove, Illinois

InterVarsity Press
P.O. Box 1400 | Downers Grove, IL 60515-1426
ivpress.com | email@ivpress.com

©2025 Michael Eugene Huerter

All rights reserved. No part of this book may be reproduced in any form without written permission from InterVarsity Press.

InterVarsity Press® is the publishing division of InterVarsity Christian Fellowship/USA®. For more information, visit intervarsity.org.

Scripture quotations, unless otherwise noted, are from the New Revised Standard Version, Updated Edition. Copyright © 2021 National Council of Churches of Christ in the United States of America. Used by permission. All rights reserved worldwide.

While any stories in this book are true, some names and identifying information may have been changed to protect the privacy of individuals.

The publisher cannot verify the accuracy or functionality of website URLs used in this book beyond the date of publication.

Cover design: Faceout Studio, Spencer Fuller
Interior design: Jeanna Wiggins
Images: Getty Images: © Kativ / E+ © Erica Shires / The Image Bank
   © Blaise Hayward / DigitalVision © Gina Pricope / Moment
   © ExperienceInteriors / E+

ISBN 978-1-5140-1142-3 (print) | ISBN 978-1-5140-1143-0 (digital)

Printed in the United States of America ∞

> **Library of Congress Cataloging-in-Publication Data**
> A catalog record for this book is available from the Library of Congress.

30 29 28 27 26 25 | 10 9 8 7 6 5 4 3 2 1

**To my parents,
Joachim and Nancy,**

*who have loved and
supported me through it all,*

**and to my mentor
Geoff Twigg,**

*who inspired me with his
theological thoughtfulness and
encouraged me on my journey
to becoming a music minister.*

Contents

Acknowledgments	ix
Introduction	1
1 Enter the Internet	23
2 Activity and Embodiment	46
3 Mediation and Virtuality	77
4 Hybridity and Church Music	109
5 Online Ritual Communities	123
Conclusion: Where Did We Come From? Where Do We Go?	149
Appendix: Live Chat Responses on ZeplaHQ's Twitch.tv Stream and YouTube Comments on Related Music Videos	157
Bibliography	161
Index	173

Acknowledgments

THIS BOOK IS THE PRODUCT OF YEARS OF STUDY, reflection, and experience—not only my own, but of many people whose work, insights, and care have made it possible. As I reflect on the relationships that have undergirded this work, prepared and supported me throughout, and shaped me as a minister and a scholar, I am grateful. Many individuals and communities have given encouragement, resources, and meaning to this journey. The true subject of this book is connection in a changing world; it could only have come about through the connections that gave me life during the many changes in my world over the past five years.

I am grateful to the Baylor faculty who gave their expertise, energy, and encouragement to my scholarship. I want to thank Monique Ingalls for her thought-expanding teaching, for advising the dissertation that would lay the groundwork for this book, and for her consistent support of this project. She has had a profound impact on my formation as a scholar. Thanks also to Randall Bradley, Maria Monteiro, Matthew Laube, Terry York, and Angela Gorrell for their significant contributions to my education and this research.

Thanks to Calvary Baptist Church for providing meaningful community and grounding my theological reflections in the life of the local church. I am especially grateful to the pastoral staff I worked with at Calvary: Hannah Coe, John Hunt, Ali DeHay, Kessa Payne, and Randall Bradley. Serving alongside you was a privilege and a blessing.

I am deeply thankful for the friends and family who came alongside me as I pursued this research. From my time studying at Baylor, I want to thank Breck McGough, Eric Amouzou, Nathan Myrick, Marcell Steuernagel, Shannan Baker, and Jon Snyder. You have been valued teachers, collaborators, and friends. Sara Dye, your friendship and perspective gave me precious encouragement during this journey. Brian and Elizabeth Crowder, you provided a relational and literal safe place and a home for me. Thank you both for your love and friendship, which I treasure dearly. Christopher Mack, you changed my life for the better and made this process more than bearable. I love you so much.

Introduction

THE COVID-19 PANDEMIC CAUGHT many churches flatfooted.[1] As the world reeled to respond to a new reality we did not understand, church leaders had to find new ways to do ministry. The early weeks of lockdown and quarantine in my church included canceled services, changing plans, and emergency meetings. We were ill-equipped to facilitate an immediate, complete shift to online modalities; we had neither the practical resources nor the experience we would have liked. Like many other churches, we managed the best we could—gathering church staff in an empty sanctuary in front of a small tablet on a camera stand, sending a video stream to our community sheltered in their homes.

As time went on, our approach continued to adapt and change. We gained new capacities and resources, learned new skills, and began to internalize patterns and practices of ministry that included a greater online presence. This ongoing transition took place in the midst of continuing conversations in church and culture at large about how our society was being reshaped. Working from home became a far more common practice than before. Zoom became a ubiquitous presence seemingly overnight. Popular-level theological conversations about the significance of online media and its role in our lives and our worship populated Christian newsletters and my own social media feed.

IN MEDIAS RES

From early 2020 to mid-2024, these conversations have coalesced into conferences, journal articles, and books both scholarly and practical. More faith

---

[1] In this research I will focus my attention primarily on Christian churches and faith communities/organizations in North America. I am writing from a Protestant perspective but will also engage with Catholic writers as well as scholars and practitioners from various contexts.

leaders are engaging in questions around online media than ever before. As our society at large has grappled with the realization that life is not going to return to exactly what it was before the pandemic, church leaders likewise have recognized that we are experiencing an inflection point in many of our practices and approaches. Church online is here to stay. But, while our theologies of ministry online have developed, in-depth reflection on specifically musical aspects of online ministry is lagging behind. In terms of theological and practical perspectives on music and new media, we may still be using a metaphorical tablet on a camera stand and making do with minimal resources. Disciplines such as church music studies, ethnomusicology, music philosophy, and practical theology have further to go in the area of digital media and music. This book hopes to synthesize perspectives and offer appropriate tools for our new hybrid digital environment.

This book focuses on the intersection of church music and online communication. The central question is this: What does the church need to understand about digitally mediated interactions—their history, embodied impact, and effective use—in order for individual communities and ministers to make well-informed, effective, and contextually appropriate decisions in their ministry? Ultimately, responsible engagement with online worship and digital religious rituals necessitates being aware of historical patterns of how churches have responded to technological innovation, reframing four important concepts (participation, embodiment, mediation, and virtuality), and reimagining community by attending to the specific affordances of online media. These issues will be essential to the development of music ministry in the 2020s and beyond.

I will address this question through assessing academic sources on topics of online communities and religious practices, as well as the history of communication technologies and the church's engagement with them. This research will include both prepandemic sources and those written since the advent of Covid-19. I will also engage with other musicological, ethnomusicological, philosophical, and theological sources on topics with implications relevant to digitally mediated faith practices and musical experiences. Primary sources include digital ethnography of online communities and interactions, and a series of interviews with leaders and participants involved in online communities.

This research has potential significance for the field of church music studies, as well as practical utility for ministry practitioners. To the extent that we do not engage thoughtfully and intentionally with online and hybrid practices, we may miss opportunities for meaningful ministry or engage in practices that are ineffective or have negative impact. In a world that operates on networks of digitally mediated relationships that begin online and then find expression in physical space, a local church without an online presence appropriate to its surrounding community may find it impossible to connect with that community in a mutually positive relationship. Conversely, a church that excels in online ministry and digital spaces but does so without grounding those practices theologically may gain the world but lose its soul.

This book takes a two-pronged approach, talking about hybrid congregations *and* music, not just one or the other. Worship is broader than just music, and music is one of numerous practices and rituals we value in our communities. Portions of this book will focus heavily on music, and other portions will address issues around technology, communal practices, and relationships, all of which are part of the fabric of our congregations.

A theology of hybrid worship is needed because it draws on resources not yet engaged within the literature on church music and online worship. For instance, the category of interpassivity is absent from significant works that address online worship. Robert Pfaller describes interpassivity as, rather than a delegation of *work*, a delegation of *consumption* or *enjoyment*: "a pleasant consuming attitude ... a 'passivity.' ... The *enjoyment* of something is—partly or even totally—delegated to other people or to a technical device."[2] I recently experienced interpassivity when I used my iPhone to take a photo of a projected slide during a sermon; I delegated the responsibility of remembering and internalizing the content to my device. While the relief I felt in the moment was real, I have yet to revisit that picture and reflect more deeply on its contents. Similar dynamics can arise with video recordings, written notes, or even the ways we imagine other people are thinking and feeling.

Another aspect largely absent from church music scholarship is the history of the church's engagement with technological revolutions. We are experiencing the early stages of a major revolution in the ways our society functions due to the invention and explosive evolution of the internet and online platforms. We will not fully grasp the implications of this revolution for some

---

[2]Robert Pfaller, *Interpassivity: The Aesthetics of Delegated Enjoyment* (Edinburgh: Edinburgh University Press, 2017), chapter 1. Emphasis original.

decades, but we can be better informed and more able to make sense of the maelstrom of accelerating change if we learn from history.

This book will also engage questions about embodiment, accessibility, and inclusion. The need for serious reflection on embodiment takes new form because of the advent of technology and resulting shifts in how human beings interact, build and maintain relationships, and engage with the world. The goal of this book is to highlight theological and practical tools that can aid ministers and churches as they make informed decisions about hybrid and online ministry efforts.

We need to think more carefully and critically about the interactions of online worship and spiritual formation because this combination is a relatively new development. Both the church and society at large are still grappling with the changes brought about by digital technology. It is not enough for churches to simply broadcast the way we have always done things online and expect this to be effective ministry in a mediated age. Instead, the church needs to develop new skills and understandings to connect effectively with people's life experiences. This theology of hybrid worship will equip and empower church music scholars and practitioners to think through questions of mediation, embodiment, participation, and online connections in informed ways, interface those with their own philosophy of church music and worship, and find new contextual insights to apply in their ministries.

BACKGROUND AND PURPOSE

The question addressed here is relatively complex and touches on a variety of disciplines. In asking what the church needs to understand about online interactions—their history, embodied impact, and effective use—in order for individual communities and ministers to make well-informed, effective, and contextually appropriate decisions in their ministry, I am really asking several sets of questions. The first concerns the history of digitally mediated human interactions. What actions and events led to the time we find ourselves in, when a huge portion of human society and its interactions are now channeled significantly through new media?[3] What historical patterns and trajectories are worthy of consideration as we seek to understand these new realities?

---

[3] That is, media that are created and distributed digitally.

The second set of questions concerns the relationship of online technologies to embodiment within church music and worship. How does music affect the body? How do human bodies interface with digital media and with other humans engaged in those media? Which human bodies are most affected by changes in patterns of liturgy and community-building activities? How do digital media offer opportunities or obstacles to those whose experience of embodied humanity is marginalized or disadvantaged?

Finally, given the historical patterns and issues raised by embodiment, what are good, beneficial, equitable, and positive ways for churches to engage with digital media, which (like all humanly created tools) also carry a potential for malformation and harm? How might the church use these tools for the kingdom of God, and to what degree can the negative aspects of these technologies be ameliorated? How does the use of new media apply across various contexts?

These questions are existential concerns for the future of the church. Christian leaders, particularly those within church music, need to grapple with questions about online media and Christian formation if we are to have meaningful contributions to make to the world. We are living in the midst of a turning point in human history, when society is being reshaped to a similar degree as in the Reformation and Counter-Reformation following the invention of the printing press. Sometimes called the Third Industrial Revolution or the digital revolution, this shift can be traced to the mid- to late twentieth century and has accelerated in the early decades of the twenty-first.[4] We still do not clearly see what we are becoming—as individuals, as communities, as the global church. This historical moment calls for serious consideration and careful thought. While every local church community and individual believer will have a unique relationship with digital media, all of us are affected to some degree by its ubiquitous presence.

Because of my own background, connections, and resources, this research will focus partly on communities based in the continental United States, and also partly on online communities spanning a variety of locations across the globe. As a Millennial pastor and music minister, I have grown up with online technology and social media being a huge part of my life experience

---

[4] Richard Hodson, "Digital Revolution," *Nature* 563, no. 7733 (2018): S131.

and personal formation; for better and for worse, engaging with digital spaces is something I do constantly, often without much conscious thought. But our cultural moment calls for intentional reflection. Without it, we will each default to our unexamined assumptions about what these technologies are and what is possible to accomplish through their use. While some might argue that churches should *not* have hybrid forms, and others may say they should immediately apply every new technological fad, I propose a middle way (a via media, if you will). Our lives are hybrid—online and offline—and our ministry must reflect this. If we are to minister in a world woven through with digital threads and relationships, we cannot afford either to embrace every aspect of digital life unquestioningly (this would neglect the countercultural call of discipleship) or to reject and dismiss opportunities these technologies offer (forgetting the presence and power of God to bring forth goodness and life in every situation). These human inventions are neither perfect nor depraved; as believers and ministers, we must seek spiritual discernment, not reactionary thinking.

An important methodology for understanding online relationships is digital ethnography. This approach to research allows for careful examination of online interactions, media, and communities. By necessity, I practiced digital ethnography within communities that make significant use of digital media and online technology.

I want to make clear at the outset that while I fully believe that there are significant social and moral problems implicated in the growth of digital media, I chose to undertake this research with the goal of finding and highlighting positive expressions of personal formation and communal interactions through new media. My intention was to explore how and to what extent this technology can be a force for good, and what approaches and safeguards are conducive to positive outcomes for ministry. I did not intend to erase or ignore the problematic sides of online interactions, but I also did not delve into the worst the internet has to offer or argue that digital media are a profound theological evil. This research was also intended to explore implications for the church's music in particular; while I engaged sources from various fields such as psychology, sociology, philosophy, and theology, the overall aim was to bring these various threads together to contribute to the field of church music studies.

SIGNIFICANCE FOR CHURCH MUSIC STUDIES AND PRACTICE

This book offers three major resources to church music scholars and practitioners. First, engaging with the history of the internet as a technological revolution highlights the parallels between various significant transitions in church music across time. By paying close attention to this history, even beyond what is addressed in these pages, we can be better informed and prepared to show up in our present cultural environment with a clear perception and vision for the future.

Second, naming the dichotomies of active and passive participation, embodied and disembodied experience, mediated and unmediated worship, and virtuality and reality is an important framework for religious thinkers and practitioners to engage with as our communities continue to seek understanding of the world-altering transitions we are living through in the twenty-first century. Adding interdisciplinary perspectives and greater nuance to these categories—and highlighting the necessity of clearly naming what is meant by each of these—will help to deepen and broaden the ongoing conversation around hybrid church practices. Rather than defaulting to reactionary responses that privilege "the way we've always done things," this framework opens greater opportunities to dig underneath unquestioned assumptions and unearth new possibilities.

Third, presenting a variety of online communities, even outside typical religious structures, as models for what is possible in online community formation is an important step forward for the field of church music studies. The field will benefit from continuing reflection and attentive study around how music actually functions in the everyday lives of people, not limiting our scholarship to only the eleven o'clock hour on Sundays. Church music studies can and should be a field that considers broader expressions of meaning-making and communal rituals and brings insights from those expressions to bear on what our churches and liturgies may become.[5]

---

[5] Mark James Porter, *Contemporary Worship Music and Everyday Musical Lives*, Ashgate Congregational Music Studies (London: Routledge, 2017).

METHODS AND SOURCES

This research engages with a significant number of sources across multiple disciplines. These sources provide a well-rounded perspective on a variety of topics that are important to consider before forming strategies and best practices for utilizing digital technologies in ministry. To understand the complex relationship between the church and technology, I bring together multiple literatures, ethnographic research, and interviews with scholars and practitioners in the field.

Digital ethnography is sometimes also called virtual fieldwork. Timothy J. Cooley, Katherine Meizel, and Nasir Syed write, "Virtual fieldwork employs technologically communicated realities in the gathering of information for ethnographic research.... Virtual fieldwork is a means of studying real people."[6] Digital ethnography as a methodology challenges "the polemic binary between 'virtual' and 'real' in the way we conduct our fieldwork, [and seeks] to understand technologies of communications as human constructions that are as real as any other human cultural production."[7] Liz Przybylski writes, "Now, [ethnography] also requires a critical skill set to tell an analytical story that makes sense of all the documents, data, and experiences available to ethnographers. This means having a strong methodology that cuts across both digital and physical field spaces."[8] Given the subject matter of this research, an approach that includes digital methods is essential.

The digital ethnography will focus on three differing online communities that have made effective use of online platforms for building relationships and meaningful, formative experiences. First, a video game stream of the massively multiplayer online roleplaying game *Final Fantasy XIV* has been mobilized to contribute funds to charities in Ukraine, and the streamer, who previously lived in Ukraine, was supported emotionally and practically by her online community when she had to flee her home under threat of invasion. Second, listeners gathered around the popular podcast *Harry Potter and the Sacred Text* have grown into a community that shares common spiritual practices, offers blessings and prayers for their

---

[6]Timothy J. Cooley, Katherine Meizel, and Nasir Syed, "Virtual Fieldwork," in *Shadows in the Field: New Perspectives for Fieldwork in Ethnomusicology*, 2nd ed., ed. Gregory F. Barz and Timothy J. Cooley (New York: Oxford University Press, 2008), 91.
[7]Cooley, Meizel, and Syed, "Virtual Fieldwork," 92.
[8]Liz Przybylski, *Hybrid Ethnography: Online, Offline, and in Between* (Los Angeles: Sage, 2020), 3.

community, and joins in remembrance of lost loved ones to offer solidarity in grief. This online community has found expression in local groups that meet to read together and advocate for various justice issues. Third, a small group of music listeners and artists have supported a songwriter named Spencer LaJoye on the website Patreon, which allows LaJoye to share meaningful reflections on their creative process and invite patrons into embodied spiritual practices.

I also interview leaders, thinkers, and ministers who are engaging with digital media in their work relating to the church. Since I am exploring topics that gained significance and attention in the past few years, there is value in speaking with people with meaningful expertise directly. To this end, I conducted eight interviews with scholars and practitioners whose areas of focus overlapped with my research. Each interview was largely conversational, and questions and topics of conversation were tailored to each interviewee's work and expertise. These eight conversation partners provided invaluable insights and shaped my thinking, and these oral sources will be a valuable supplement to the written literature. It will be helpful to introduce each interviewee briefly, with a description of their work and its relevance to this research.

Heidi A. Campbell is a professor and scholar at Texas A&M University specializing in digital media, culture, and religion. She directs the Network for New Media, Religion and Digital Culture Studies. Her work has been influential in establishing the field of digital religion studies, which Campbell describes as engaging "how not only people practice religion in digital spaces and mediated online spaces but also how those practices and the trends within digital culture impact church more broadly."[9] Campbell's scholarship and edited works constitute a significant contribution to the field.

Rev. Taylor Burton-Edwards is director of Ask the UMC, is a former director of worship resources at the United Methodist Church's General Board of Discipleship, and also does ecumenical work between denominations, being a rostered minister of Word and sacrament in the Evangelical Lutheran Church in America. Burton-Edwards offers a broad and valuable perspective on what a large swath of local churches were doing regarding online worship during the Covid-19 pandemic, as well as demographic information.

---

[9]Heidi A. Campbell, interview by author, Zoom, January 20, 2023.

Joe Iovino serves as director of member communications for United Methodist Communications and oversees the denominational website www.umc.org. As part of his position, Iovino works to provide worship resources for United Methodist churches and has been involved in the United Methodist Church's efforts to navigate transitions to online worship efforts. Iovino has had firsthand experience of the challenges inherent in these transitions and the obstacles faced by local churches and the denomination as a whole.

Father Lorenzo Lebrija is the chief innovation officer of Virginia Theological Seminary and also serves as executive director of an organization called TryTank Experimental Lab. TryTank experiments with implementing new ideas for innovative practices in the church. Before he began this work, Lebrija served the Episcopal Diocese of Los Angeles as chief development officer. Lebrija brings a flexible theological imagination and a willingness to try new things to the challenges facing the church today.

Allison Norton is a researcher and co-investigator with the Exploring the Pandemic Impact on Congregations project. Exploring the Pandemic Impact on Congregations is conducted by the Hartford Institute for Religion Research at Hartford International University and is funded by Lilly Endowment. Norton is a part of the faculty of the Hartford Institute for Religion Research, which began a five-year longitudinal study in 2021. Exploring the Pandemic Impact on Congregations is a collaborative, ecumenical effort that uses both qualitative and quantitative data. Norton provides fascinating and compelling data about the trajectory of online, offline, and hybrid worship practices in the American church, as well as qualitative observations about why people choose to engage with online rituals and how they experience those rituals.

Rev. Pete Phillips is the program director of the master of arts in digital theology at Spurgeon's College, the head of digital theology at Premiere Christian Media, and honorary research fellow in theology and religion at Durham University. He is an advocate for hybrid ministry and worship practices and focuses his work on lived practices and theologies of digital religion. Phillips offers incisive reflection on the presuppositions many people in the church bring to digital practices as well as creative and deeply thoughtful theological insights.

DJ Soto is a pastor working in virtual reality spaces. He is a member of the governing board of Metaverse Church and serves as bishop of Virtual Reality Church and MMO Church.[10] Soto has been doing ministry in virtual reality since 2016 and offers an entrepreneurial spirit and a practitioner's perspective on innovative expressions of ministry using digital technology.

Laryssa Whittaker is lecturer in anthropology of audiences and user research lead at StoryFutures. StoryFutures is a government-funded research center based at Royal Holloway, University of London, that focuses on virtual reality and augmented reality technologies. Whittaker has conducted research on virtual reality, metaverse, and hybrid concerts in the United Kingdom, as well as surveys of people who attend virtual and livestream musical events. Whittaker also contributes thought-provoking correctives to stereotypes about virtual reality and metaverse experiences and the people who engage with them.

This combination of methods offers a meaningful contribution to the field on the topic of online worship. All these resources will be useful as we move forward in developing hybrid ministry models that make use of both offline and online modalities. These sources have been chosen based on their relevance to questions around embodied, emotionally salient, communal interactions with identifiable impact on personal formation. Therefore, this work requires developing preliminary criteria for evaluating online interactions in terms of their effectiveness in discipleship. The logic behind this research is that some religious groups were already engaging significantly in online spaces prior to the pandemic, while others have adopted online worship since the pandemic, and we can learn from their successes and failures. Nonreligious groups have found ways to make highly effective use of various online platforms, and their experiences may provide important insights from which the church can benefit.

THE PURPOSES OF THIS BOOK

How Christian scholars and practitioners understand and experience online community will inform the ways they try to engage with or facilitate it. This book proposes theoretical and methodological approaches that can inform a

---

[10] "Metaverse Board—VR Church in the Metaverse," VR MMO Church, accessed May 24, 2023, www.vrchurch.org/board.

variety of substantive expressions, depending on the context and priorities of the community in question. The goal is to inform, equip, and provoke thought leading to action, not to prescribe specifics. You will not read this book and find ten easy steps to a successful online ministry or worship service; instead, I hope you will be inspired to think deeply and carefully about worship, community, and online interactions.

This book has the potential to be beneficial both to scholars in the intersection of disciplines implicated in church music studies, and to church leaders and ministry practitioners. At the time of this writing, there has been little work within the field of church music that provides sustained interdisciplinary reflection on new questions raised by the digital revolution and highlighted in recent years by the Covid-19 pandemic. Scholars may find helpful connections or ideas from which to ground further research. I hope to facilitate these connections by drawing on interdisciplinary sources and contributing new synthesis of sources not yet taken advantage of in existing literature. Church leaders and church music practitioners may gain useful information, perspectives, and approaches to direct and improve their ministry efforts.

This book will provide more nuanced and precise concepts for discussing and understanding digital religious practices, especially within the context of musical worship. These concepts have the potential to correct misconceptions about digital realities and present additional perspectives that look for the positive potential in online interactions, while not disregarding their shortcomings. I hope scholars will apply this book to engage in productive interdisciplinary conversations around digital culture, worship, and community building. It can also be a resource for churches to approach online and hybrid ministries with greater intentionality and clarity.

TURNING POINTS IN MEDIA ECOLOGIES

As I approach the question of how churches can reflect on and engage with online media in positive ways, I want to place our current cultural moment in a broader context. The Covid-19 pandemic was a catalyst for major change in churches' worship practices; however, the threat of viral spread arguably only accelerated a process of transformation that was already taking place. The world was already changing, and Christian music and worship can benefit from gaining greater understanding of that change.

Historically, when the church encounters new technologies, its responses follow consistent patterns. Catholic scholar of liturgical studies and theologian Teresa Berger remarks on the dynamics appearing in the twenty-first century around digital media. She places them in the context of other technologies throughout history: "Digital media stand in a long line of human creations that repeat similar patterns. That said, digital media, because of the vast advances in technology, exacerbate . . . some of the good and some of the really vicious potential that is always there in human beings coming together in startling ways. And we have seen both over the years."[11] Of course, there are also dynamics that are unique to each time, place, and technology; however, these patterns are significant and can prove useful in our reckoning with the rapid change we are experiencing in the twenty-first century.

In her introduction to the edited volume *Congregational Music-Making and Community in a Mediated Age*, Anna Nekola writes, "Media technologies may affect us, but rather than seeing media technology as acting upon us and shaping us, we must instead examine the complex interactive world where people create technologies for certain ends and use technologies in ways that always have important social and political implications."[12] Every time a new communication technology appears and begins to affect society, there is a dual response of excitement and anxiety. New questions arise about what it means to be human in a changing world, how the technologies we shape are in turn reshaping us. Our relationships, our social institutions, our theologies, and even the basic structures of our cognition are transformed. Sometimes these transformations are subtle; other times a new technology profoundly disturbs our presuppositions and demands that we explore new perspectives. Each new technology also interacts with the surrounding culture, religious and governmental structures, and previous forms of technology. In some cases, these interactions are surprising and challenging to navigate. One form of communication technology may come to dominate society and diminish the role of the others. Alternatively, a new technology

---

[11] Teresa Berger, "Digital Devotion: Christianity Online," October 11, 2017, in *The Quadcast*, podcast, https://soundcloud.com/yaleuniversity/the-quadcast-digital-devotion-christianity-online.

[12] Anna E. Nekola, "Introduction: Worship Media as Media Form and Mediated Practice: Theorizing the Intersections of Media, Music and Lived Religion," in *Congregational Music-Making and Community in a Mediated Age*, ed. Anna E. Nekola and Thomas Wagner (Farnham, UK: Routledge, 2015), 8.

may become enmeshed with an existing pattern or tool, enabling new possibilities for both.[13]

It may not be fully possible to grasp the scope and impact of a technological revolution we are still in the midst of; however, scholars and practitioners in the church have a responsibility to provide our communities with the best tools we can. These tools will help each of our communities navigate these uncharted waters with greater clarity and confidence. They will not eliminate the challenges we face but will better equip us to move forward faithfully and wisely in contextually appropriate ways. Context is key, as media always function within the cultural environment, or ecology, in which they are used.

Tom Wagner suggests studying music as "both a media object and a form of media," using the framework of "media ecology." Wagner describes media ecology as "the study of how dominant forms of communication in a media environment affect the ways people relate to the world."[14] Media ecology acknowledges the close and essential connections between media and environments; they are constitutive of each other and profoundly influence each other.[15] In this framework, every form of media exists as part of a larger system, a multimedia environment. The technologies of language, symbolic meaning, and mechanical and cultural processes—such as print, radio, television, digital media, music, and other forms of mediation—interact in dynamic ways within this environment.[16] In one sense, media *are* environments.

These media are both *sensorial*—meaning they both engage and shape the ways we use our senses—and *symbolic*—a system with assigned meanings, logic, and syntax that requires a degree of aptitude. Whichever media are dominant will shape human senses, the unwritten rules of interaction, and our individual and collective perceptions of reality. Wagner understands congregational music as a form of media in itself, one that is culturally coded.

---

[13]Nekola and Wagner, *Congregational Music-Making and Community*; Teresa Berger, *@ Worship: Liturgical Practices in Digital Worlds*, Liturgy, Worship, and Society (New York: Routledge, 2018); Heidi A. Campbell and John Dyer, eds., *Ecclesiology for a Digital Church* (London: SCM Press, 2021).

[14]Tom Wagner, "Music as Mediated Object, Music as Medium: Towards a Media Ecological View of Congregational Music," in Nekola and Wagner, *Congregational Music-Making and Community*, 25, 27.

[15]Wagner, "Music as Mediated Object," 29.

[16]Wagner, "Music as Mediated Object," 29.

Introduction

He suggests, "The way congregational music is 'understood' requires familiarity with the cultural codes that give it meaning in a given context. . . . The relative mastery of these codes, especially in the actual making of music, has implications for who can participate and how."[17] Music is a media form with its own grammar, and this grammar is changing as culture, musical genres, and media technologies shift around us. The huge changes brought about by the internet mean that the grammar of music has changed as well, having profound implications for who can participate and how. The language of church music is shifting in response to the accelerated changes in the world around us, and we will need to learn how to speak anew.

The frame of media ecology invites us to imagine culture and media as parts of an ecosystem with various species, weather and climate patterns, and resources. Just as the introduction of a nonnative species or the reintroduction of a native organism can literally reshape the landscape of a natural environment, the interactions of various media have profound and sometimes unpredictable effects on human society and experience. As Wagner puts it, "New technologies reorient the way their predecessors and other technologies are used and valued in relation to one another, culture and society. Furthermore, they reorient the ideologies, values and structures of the culture itself."[18]

In order to understand how various media technologies have reshaped the world, the church, and church music, it is helpful to take a media-ecological approach to considering rituals and formative practices. This kind of approach "understands congregational music as a technology, in the widest sense of the term, which influences values, religious sensitivities and basic theological understandings."[19]

This ecological approach helps to highlight the turmoil that has arisen time and time again for the church with new technologies and media forms. The radio raised concerns about how the listening public would relate to musical performance. Would they still travel or pay to see live music performed when they could listen at home? Would they learn to play instruments themselves anymore? Questions also arose around the efficacy of radio

---

[17] Wagner, "Music as Mediated Object," 29-30.
[18] Wagner, "Music as Mediated Object," 31.
[19] Wagner, "Music as Mediated Object," 39.

ministry compared to familiar models. Were preaching and music ministry mediated through the radio spiritually legitimate and able to lead to transformation? How would ministers adapt to the new environment, and what would happen to those who failed to shift their approach?[20]

The television brought about anxieties regarding the relationship of the "electronic church" to local faith communities. Would conservative independent preachers gain an outsized influence and push out mainline religious groups? How would the parasocial nature of the viewers' relationships with those preachers affect religious communities? There were serious questions in the early years of television about whether worship was even possible through televised music. Would such offerings be legitimate and authentic?[21]

The dynamics of media ecologies have appeared in multiple historical moments. Each developing technology has influenced the values, religious sensitivities, and theological understandings of believers attempting to leverage it for ministry. If this is the case, how will the technology that is congregational music interact with new technologies such as social media and streaming services?

The historical trajectories of the radio and television have lessons to teach us. Each one was disruptive in its early years, bringing new questions to the surface that were previously unimaginable. Each one eventually came to be naturalized as a normal part of society and of the church. If the advents of these technologies were significant inflection points in culture and the development and dissemination of church music, other, newer technologies such

---

[20]See Mark Ward, *The Lord's Radio: Gospel Music Broadcasting and the Making of Evangelical Culture, 1920–1960* (Jefferson, NC: McFarland, 2017); Robert H. Lochte, *Christian Radio: The Growth of a Mainstream Broadcasting Force* (Jefferson, NC: McFarland, 2006); Peter Elvy and Jerusalem Trust, *Opportunities and Limitations in Religious Broadcasting* (Edinburgh: Centre for Theology and Public Issues, 1991); Lyle W. Dorsett, *Billy Sunday and the Redemption of Urban America* (Grand Rapids, MI: Eerdmans, 1991); Mark Ward, *Air of Salvation: The Story of Christian Broadcasting* (Grand Rapids, MI: Baker Books, 1994); Hal Erickson, *Religious Radio and Television in the United States, 1921–1991: The Programs and Personalities* (Jefferson, NC: McFarland, 1992).

[21]See Everett C. Parker, *Religious Television; What to Do and How* (New York: Harper, 1961); Peter G. Horsfield, *Religious Television: The American Experience* (New York: Longman, 1984); Stewart M. Hoover, *Mass Media Religion: The Social Sources of the Electronic Church* (Newbury Park, CA: Sage, 1988); Janice Peck, *The Gods of Televangelism* (Cresskill, NJ: Hampton, 1993); Alf Linderman, *The Reception of Religious Television: Social Semeiology Applied to an Empirical Case Study* Acta Universitatis Upsaliensis, Psychologia et Sociologia Religionum 12 (Uppsala: S. Academiae Ubsaliensis, 1996).

as the internet and social media certainly signal equally important paradigm shifts. How will churches engage this new landscape, and what potentialities and perils await us there? Churches must grapple with questions about their own worship practices, rituals, and sacraments in light of increasing digital mediatization of church services in the wake of the Covid-19 pandemic.

Our own new technologies will doubtless shape the ways we compose, experience, and share music. We are still discovering what we are becoming in light of the internet and related technologies that are transforming our world. The internet is a powerful tool, and humanity's future in the era of digital technologies and connections is still taking shape. The history of prior technological revolutions offers insights and questions to bring to these concerns, but the answers we are living and discovering may surprise us.

CHAPTER OUTLINE

Chapter one, "Enter the Internet," explores the technocultural revolution brought about by the internet and digital technologies. The internet has become a ubiquitous presence in much of human life, and it profoundly influences much of what we do and who we are. This technology also has brought about a new kind of economy, sometimes called the "attention economy." Drawing on Justin E. H. Smith's description of the necessity of "transformative moral commitment" in light of an economy that compromises and capitalizes on human attention, and combining this perspective with Martin Buber's theological work on the "I-Thou" stance in spiritual life, I propose a way forward for formative use of church music that uses internet technologies.

The following two chapters will engage with perceived dichotomies that frequently appear in conversations around online and hybrid ministry expressions. Online worship is often assumed to be passive, disembodied, mediated, and virtual. This is sometimes contrasted with active, embodied, unmediated, real engagement in worship, which is held up as the ideal of church music and thought to be possible only in physical gatherings.

Chapter two, "Activity and Embodiment," addresses two of these issues. The first of these pairs contrasts active with passive engagement. Active participation is often a major focus for worship leaders, and this kind of communal engagement appears, at least initially, to be hindered by digital practices. For the church to see productive ways forward by engaging these technologies, it will benefit from reexamining the value of activity, passivity, and the various kinds of connection made possible along this spectrum. Active participation in worship is idealized in contrast to passivity, which is typically viewed in a negative light. Robert Pfaller's work on interpassivity offers a useful corrective to this binary approach.[22]

The second topic of this chapter is embodiment, and along with that, the assumption of online activities as disembodied. Online or digital interactions are frequently termed disembodied, and it is therefore necessary to explore the bodily aspects both of online experiences and of musicking.[23] The question of embodiment will also touch on concerns of accessibility and inclusion, as the language often used around embodiment cloaks the reality that existing patterns of worship practice fail to value and include many bodies.[24] Examining the significance of embodiment in light of the Covid-19 pandemic and the resulting shift toward more online worship raises important questions about the physical contours of our established systems and practices, and requires us to consider whose embodiment is served by those systems and practices.

Chapter three, "Mediation and Virtuality," gives attention to the second two sets of issues. The third dichotomy is the distinction between mediated and unmediated experience. Worship is sometimes idealized as an unmediated encounter with God;[25] I will show this is not the case and propose

---

[22]Pfaller, *Interpassivity*. Carolyn J. Mackie helpfully expands Pfaller's category of interpassivity into religious categories in "Believing for Me: Žižek, Interpassivity, and Christian Experience" (paper presented at Institute for Christian Studies, May 2, 2013).

[23]Ken Hillis, *Digital Sensations: Space, Identity, and Embodiment in Virtual Reality*, Electronic Mediations 1 (Minneapolis: University of Minnesota Press, 1999); Ken McAnally and Guy Wallis, "Visual-Haptic Integration, Action and Embodiment in Virtual Reality," *Psychological Research* 86, no. 6 (2021): 1847-57; Peter Phillips, "Digital Being," *Crucible*, January 2023, https://crucible.hymnsam.co.uk/articles/2023/january/articles/digital-being/; Ramón Pelinski, "Embodiment and Musical Experience," *Trans* 9 (2005), www.sibetrans.com/trans/articulo/178/embodiment-and-musical-experience; Eugene Montague, "Entrainment and Embodiment in Musical Performance," in *The Oxford Handbook of Music and the Body*, ed. Youn Kim and Sander L. Gilman (Oxford: Oxford University Press, 2019), 177-92; Hamish Robb, "Imagined, Supplemental Sound in Nineteenth-Century Piano Music: Towards a Fuller Understanding of Musical Embodiment," *Music Theory Online* 21, no. 3 (2015), https://mtosmt.org/issues/mto.15.21.3/mto.15.21.3.robb.html.

[24]Amy Kenny, *My Body Is Not a Prayer Request: Disability Justice in the Church* (Grand Rapids, MI: Baker Books, 2022).

[25]An important resource on the topic of mediation is Berger's *@ Worship*. Berger convincingly argues that worship has always involved mediation, regardless of which technologies were being used.

Introduction

a theological understanding of mediation as a positive good and an essential part of the relationship we have with God in Christ, rather than an obstacle to connection.[26]

The fourth dichotomy is between the virtual and the real. The terminology of *virtual* has its own trajectory of transformation in scholarly conversations over the past several decades, and it is important to acknowledge the limitations of this framing and to recognize the intermingling of various expressions of human culture and relationships, whether digital or not. Examining the real impacts of virtual experiences and their practical expression in the world invites further reflection on things often dismissed as "unreal."[27] This section will also explore the potential of virtual reality community, rituals, and music, and the moral impact of virtual reality experiences.

These four topics do not represent an exhaustive list of necessary questions for the church in the age of the internet. However, engaging with them will provide ample opportunity to reflect on important dynamics as the church continues to move forward. Participation, embodiment, mediation, and virtuality are crucial to meaningful conversation about online ministry. Many, if not nearly all, of the questions arising in churches about the new online landscape can be considered from one or more of these perspectives.

Chapter four, "Hybridity and Church Music," synthesizes scholarly perspectives on the intermingling of online and offline realities in a world that has increasingly internalized the internet and digital technologies. As society continues to integrate digital technology more fully into everyday life, it is no longer possible or productive to draw a firm dividing line between online and offline—the two spheres overlap now more than ever. Faith in a hybrid world requires learning how to integrate these spheres of our life, and faith communities' worship through church music is one expression of that

---

Georgina Born's research on mediation in music is also instrumental in this research. Joshua Busman, Monique Ingalls, Miranda Klaver, and Richard Grusin offer important perspectives on mediation.

[26] Richard Grusin, "Radical Mediation," *Critical Inquiry* 42, no. 1 (2015): 124-48; Berger, @ *Worship*.

[27] Fernanda Herrera, "Virtual Embodiment and Embodied Cognition: Effect of Virtual Reality Perspective Taking Tasks on Empathy and Prejudice," in *A Multidisciplinary Approach to Embodiment: Understanding Human Being*, ed. Nancy Kimberly Dess (New York: Routledge, 2021), 127-32; Rachel Wagner, *Godwired: Religion, Ritual, and Virtual Reality*, Media, Religion, and Culture (London: Routledge, 2012); Benjamin J. Chicka, *Playing as Others: Theology and Ethical Responsibility in Video Games* (Waco, TX: Baylor University Press, 2021).

integration.[28] Realities of increasing hybridity invite scholars and practitioners of church music to revisit and reconsider *why* we make music together, what it means, and how we can continue to do so in meaningful, loving, and God-honoring ways in a changing world. This chapter will also propose criteria for evaluating online communal practices.

Chapter five, "Online Ritual Communities," includes digital ethnography of three groups on the internet that make effective use of online technologies in meaningful ways that build community. A Twitch.tv video game stream, a podcast listening community, and a group of patrons supporting a songwriter and communicating with them and each other online all display the positive potential of communal practices online. This chapter will look at these online communities, the platforms they choose to use, and the advantages and disadvantages of those media. These examples provide opportunity for considering the implications and potential impact of digital media platforms on community formation and church music practice in a world of hybrid ministry. Our churches can learn important lessons from people and groups who better understand and use these technologies than our church leaders have to this point.

The conclusion, "Where Did We Come From? Where Do We Go?," will situate this book in the broader conversation of church music studies. I offer reflections on the significance of this research for the field and note some of the many potential areas that call for further study.

The goal of this research is not to solve all problems related to these topics with any finality but to open up conversation and introduce productive questions and connections that can lead to new insights, both within and beyond this book.

As the Covid-19 pandemic transformed our experience of church and faith community, I found myself doing whatever I could think to do to care for my church. I knew we had to *do something*, and so I threw myself into the work. Sunday was still coming, and our congregants still needed community, invitation into Christian disciplines, and worship. Ministry in a crisis galvanized

---

[28] Angela Gorrell, *Always On: Practicing Faith in a New Media Landscape*, Theology for the Life of the World (Grand Rapids, MI: Baker Academic, 2019); Heidi A. Campbell and John Dyer, eds., *Ecclesiology for a Digital Church* (London: SCM Press, 2021); August E. Grant et al., *Religion Online: How Digital Technology Is Changing the Way We Worship and Pray* (Santa Barbara, CA: Praeger, 2019).

new approaches and creativity. However, I soon realized that triage was not enough. Our pressing, urgent problems revealed deeper shifts that called for sustained research and reflection, not only stopgap solutions. This book is my contribution to interested conversation about the church's life and worship in an age of digital media.[29] It is the expression of my love for the church and my hope for the future of God's dream for the world, whatever lies ahead of us.

---

[29]Gorrell emphasizes the need for "interested conversation" in online faith practices in *Always On*, 33-35.

Enter the Internet

SEVERAL PASTORS I HAVE WORKED with have remarked, with varying degrees of humor and exasperation, how rarely congregants seem to remember the content of their sermons. They have also named the felt struggle of inviting a community to the renewing of their minds in following Christ when this community is gathered for perhaps a few hours one day of the week, and the rest of the week is bombarded with constant messaging, advertising, and news stories apparently designed to fuel our demons, not summon our best selves: "How can a weekly church service compete with this environment inundated by greed, fear, anger, and injustice?"

These concerns are not limited to the age of the internet; they have been the challenge of ministry for a long, long time. It is worth recognizing that these forces are connected to economic models that seek to generate profit and power. The love of money is the root of each of these kinds of evil, and these voices clamor for our attention constantly. Directing our attention elsewhere and stepping outside the rushing current of the temptations Christ faced in the desert—toward consumption, influence, and possessions—is a central practice of discipleship and worship. This has remained true throughout the history of the church, but these age-old questions require fresh examination in our new media environment.

Just as previous communication technologies reshaped human relationships, institutions, and self-understanding, the internet has become a driving force in human society in recent decades. Our personal lives and our communities; the ways we communicate, share news, and do business; the challenges faced by institutions, governments, and nations; global economies and sociological changes affecting billions of people—all have been affected profoundly by the internet. To understand what churches are facing in regard to their music ministry online, it is crucial to begin with an understanding of some of these powerful currents and events.

I will begin this chapter by describing broader cultural impacts of the internet. I will continue by bringing philosophical and theological scholarship to bear on the significance of these changes. Once that groundwork is laid, I will focus more specifically on church music and the changes and challenges brought about in that sphere by the internet. Here I will share insights from personal interviews with scholars and ministry practitioners. Finally, I will synthesize and propose a way forward for church music, based on the content of this chapter.

ATTENTION, PLEASE!

Picture this scene: A dark room is lit by a slowly turning array of green stars. A blue spotlight illuminates a man wearing a white T-shirt and sunglasses, seated at a keyboard. He begins to play and sing:

> Welcome to the Internet
> Have a look around
> Anything that brain of yours can think of can be found . . .
> Could I interest you in everything?
> All of the time?[1]

Bo Burnham's 2021 Netflix comedy special *Bo Burnham: Inside* is a curious glimpse into the mind of a White, male, Millennial comedian who is hyperaware of and reflective on the oddities and perils of the internet. *Inside* was filmed by Burnham in his home, with no film crew or audience, over the first year of the Covid-19 pandemic and reflects on numerous aspects of Burnham's experience of lockdown. It has received numerous awards, and this musical number, "Welcome to the Internet," has over 143 million views on YouTube in addition to Netflix streams. "Welcome to the Internet" positions Burnham as a personification of the internet itself, or perhaps an amalgam of Silicon Valley tech moguls and media corporations with a generous pinch of dramatically animated Disney villain thrown in.

---

[1] Bo Burnham, "Welcome to the Internet—Bo Burnham (from 'Inside'—ALBUM OUT NOW)," June 4, 2021, video, 4:40, www.youtube.com/watch?v=k1BneeJTDcU.

The song highlights many of the problems and concerns raised by the internet: the chaotic juxtaposition of bubbly, happy content with virtual front-row seats to worldwide tragedy and violence; the online pornography industry and other exploitative uses of the medium; the dizzying overwhelm of constant stimulation and access to more information than we will ever make sense of; and the impact on children's mental and social formation as they grow up in a world so different from what their parents experienced.

On January 9, 2019, Bo Burnham was part of a panel discussion hosted by the Child Mind Institute on the topic "Self-Esteem in the Age of Social Media." The conversation touched on the psychological well-being of children and adults but also grappled with the economic systems at play in a world defined by social media. Burnham remarked, "We used to colonize land. That was the thing you could expand into, and that's where money was to be made. We colonized the entire earth. There was no other place for the businesses and capitalism to expand into. And then they realized . . . human attention. . . . They are now trying to colonize every minute of your life."[2] Burnham is drawing attention to a profound shift in the way that global economies function in the age of the internet. This shift toward an economy that (in Burnham's words) colonizes human attention and time is a fundamental concern for thinking productively about the church's discipleship and musical practices in the twenty-first century.

The dynamics described by Burnham's comedy suggest a larger set of issues around the internet and its impact on our lives. While the internet has ushered in positive technological advancement, it has also corresponded with and contributed to cultural forces of distraction, alienation, and objectification. These dynamics are of huge importance to Christian formation and community, particularly worship. Christian worship (including music and a range of other rituals) is meant to positively direct human attention, to bring us into deeper connection with God, the world, and ourselves, and to remind us of the worth and goodness of creation. Worship invites us to seek righteousness, justice, beauty, and flourishing life for all God's creatures, and therefore runs counter to any influence toward disintegration, disconnection, or degradation.

---

[2]Child Mind Institute, "Self Esteem in the Age of Social Media," January 19, 2019, video, 55:35, www.youtube.com/watch?v=UmUm7oBqCVw.

HOW WE GOT HERE: THE INTERNET AT THE TURN OF THE MILLENNIUM

The 1990s saw the rise of a developing conversation about the internet's potentials and problems, as well as parallels with previous technologies. In 1998, Gray Young named the excitement and anxiety felt at the cusp of a new millennium. Excitement suggested great possibilities ahead: free exchange of information, greater freedoms, equality, and connection between individuals and communities around the world. Anxiety suggested a vision of "the Internet portending the downfall of civilized society" through rampant pornography, the decimation of privacy in the face of corporate and federal surveillance, the end of reliable journalism, the destruction of copyright, and violent criminals and terrorists taking advantage of the technology.[3]

These optimistic and pessimistic readings of the internet's potential have proven to accurately reflect our current reality; these are many of the same opportunities and pitfalls we encounter now. Young asked whether the internet could improve life, or whether we should perhaps be afraid it would ruin life, and how governments and businesses should and would regulate, restrict, or embrace it. Even as the internet has developed and become more inseparable from our daily lives than ever before, these questions remain salient and pressing.

The same concerns Young articulated in 1998 are crucial for us in the third decade of the twenty-first century. It is important to remember that new technologies may take decades, or even centuries, to become fully integrated into society; at the same time, new expressions of these technologies are being produced at dizzying rates. There is so much rapid change occurring, and we are far from fully understanding the revolution we are living through. Young compares the internet to a "precocious child," full of latent potential *and* capable of making foolish and dangerous choices, with political, academic, and economic leaders being analogous to young parents unsure how to encourage the former and curtail the latter. Young asks, "Will the child grow to be a Nobel Prize winner or an uncontrollably brilliant psychopath?"[4] Like the printing press, radio, and television before it, the

---

[3]Gray Young, ed., *The Internet*, The Reference Shelf 70 (New York: H. W. Wilson, 1998), vii.
[4]Young, *Internet*, vii.

internet asks of us: What will it be? Will it become a force for good or for evil in the world? How will it interact with and transform existing technologies and economies?

On February 19, 1998, George Conrades gave an address to the Institute of Electrical and Electronics Engineers that aimed to shed light on these questions. The event was the 1998 Network Operations and Management Symposium in New Orleans. Conrades was at the time president of GTE Internetworking, which would later be acquired by Bell Atlantic and go on to become Verizon. Conrades predicted that the internet, which was already indispensable to much of American society, would soon "disappear." By this he meant that, like other technologies before it, its use and constant presence would become normalized. Conrades remarked, "All successful technologies ultimately disappear. They penetrate so deeply into our environment, they become indistinguishable from it."[5]

Conrades's statements here highlight an important concept. He confirms what can be anticipated from study of earlier technological revolutions; that is, that each new communication medium goes through a period of flux, after which it stabilizes into a simultaneously more predictable and more forgettable feature of the surrounding society. The printing press seemed to threaten existing conceptions of studiousness, wisdom, and the rights of authors and composers; now printing is assumed and practically invisible. In the same way, the radio raised questions about the viability of live music performances and the future of music education; now these practices coexist with the radio and its successor in online music streaming. Likewise, the television has gradually become both ubiquitous and unremarkable.

One helpful example of how these successive technologies have developed is through the ways societies have shared news with each. Conrades claimed in 1998 that the internet was gathering and incorporating aspects of previous communication technologies (newspapers, radio, television, computers, telephones) as it gained dominance in global information sharing. The internet would not only transform the landscape of news media but would change the people and communities using it.[6]

---

[5]George Conrades, "The Future of the Internet: Predicting the Unpredictable," in Young, *Internet*, 179.
[6]Conrades, "Future of the Internet," 181.

This process of integration and transformation involved overcoming the internet's technical constraints and practical problems of infrastructure (such as bandwidth, security, and quality). Conrades claimed it would be necessary for the internet to be supremely accessible: "We will have to make the Internet as easy to use as dialing a telephone or switching channels on a remote control." This ease of use is one of three primary criteria Conrades suggested would determine the internet's success: "To make the Internet disappear, in other words, to enable it to truly succeed," other goals would need to be achieved. In addition to ease of use, the internet would need to become ubiquitous and gain a high level of trust from users, governments, and businesses. Once these goals were reached, Conrades hypothesized that technical concerns would fade into secondary status, with "new economic, political, and social challenges" coming to the forefront.[7]

The economic concerns would prove to be highly formative to the internet's development. In "A Brief History of the Internet," field descriptor Walt Howe reflects on the internet's growth and the impact of that change on business. Howe points out both the exponential growth of the internet and the chaos of businesses attempting to make the internet profitable. While profit margins for online sales of goods were low, the potential market was huge. At the same time, free online services including advertisements to generate revenue were beginning to grow.[8] How the internet was to be made profitable proved to be a question with wide-reaching implications for our society.

PAYING ATTENTION: THE ATTENTION ECONOMY

Writing in 2006, literary scholar Richard Lanham considered the economic implications of a world in which the internet had become ubiquitous. Lanham pushed back against popular conceptions of an economy driven by information. Lanham described economics as being concerned with the allocation of scarce resources to produce and distribute goods across society. Lanham argued the so-called information economy implied information was a scarce resource, and this was demonstrably not the case. Instead, the internet had brought on an overabundance of information: "We're drowning in it.

---

[7]Conrades, "Future of the Internet," 181.
[8]Walt Howe, "A Brief History of the Internet," in Young, *Internet*, 3-7.

There is too much information to make sense of it all.... What then is the new scarcity that economics seeks to describe? It can only be the human attention needed to make sense of information."[9]

In Lanham's description, the scarce resource being brokered in this new economy is attention, not information. What it means to be a thinking human being is changing once again in light of technological, social, and economic change. Information is overwhelmingly available, but deep understanding and application of that information is not.

Philosopher Justin E. H. Smith tackles this reality in his thought-provoking 2022 book *The Internet Is Not What You Think It Is*. Echoing Burnham's words about the colonization of human attention, Smith writes:

> The largest industry in the world now is quite literally the attention-seeking industry. Just as in the nineteenth and twentieth centuries the global economy was dominated by natural-resource extraction, today the world's largest companies have grown as large as they have entirely on the promise of providing to their clients the attention, however fleeting, of their billions of users.[10]

This is the economy so many of us participate in every day: one of personal data being fed into an algorithm to produce targeted advertisements intended to entice internet users into clicking links and staying engaged with online media platforms. Smith goes on to describe how the new economic model interfaces with previous arrangements and constitutes a sea change in the ways our world operates. This economic system, where the primary driving force is not our labor but our attention and data about us, is "a revolution at least as massive as the agricultural and industrial revolutions that preceded it." Smith concludes, "Whatever else happens, it is safe to say that for the rest of all of our lifetimes, we will only be living out the internal turbulence of this entry into a new historical epoch."[11] Just as previous technological revolutions featured chaotic transformation for decades and even centuries, the introduction of both new communication technologies and

---

[9]Richard A. Lanham, *The Economics of Attention: Style and Substance in the Age of Information* (Chicago: University of Chicago Press, 2006), 6-7.

[10]Justin E. H. Smith, *The Internet Is Not What You Think It Is: A History, a Philosophy, a Warning* (Princeton, NJ: Princeton University Press, 2022), 14.

[11]Smith, *Internet Is Not What You Think*, 15.

new economic models will certainly result in major changes. The growing pains will be significant.[12]

Smith highlights that this larger pattern is not unique to the internet but has occurred at multiple times throughout history. However, he does point out aspects of our current experience that are unique. First, Smith proposes that the development of the internet and the attention economy constitute "a new sort of exploitation, in which human beings are not only exploited in the use of their labor for extraction of natural resources; rather, their lives are *themselves* the resource, and they are exploited in its extraction." Second, he argues, "The emerging extractive economy threatens our ability to use our mental faculty of attention in a way that is conducive to human thriving."[13]

Whenever we find ourselves aimlessly scrolling through websites, it is not an accident; it is by design, and our distraction is being monetized. Smith suggests that human attention has been diminished by dominant expressions of new internet technologies. Proper attention, in Smith's view, involves a true openness to the object of one's attention. It may take on new and different meanings as we consider it. We may experience radical transformation through sustained attention to a piece of art, a novel, a poem, or another person. Smith argues that this form of attention is directly undercut by current models of internet media. However, he suggests that it is not the technology itself that is to blame. It is not inevitable that an abundance of information should lead to a scarcity of attention. Instead, it is the economic model that "maximizes solicitations upon a user's attention and ensures that the attention is never focused in one place for long" that is the cause of this degradation, perpetrated by "an engine that is explicitly designed to prod the would-be attender ever onward from one monetizable object to the next." Smith suggests that this economy of attention extraction calls for "the cultivation of *individual* attention," which "amounts to a form of hard-won resistance against this economy."[14]

---

[12]Smith also notes that these revolutions are not experienced in the present as stark contrasts of new innovation against old ways of ignorance but rather always as in continuity with the past (*Internet Is Not What You Think*, 81).
[13]Smith, *Internet Is Not What You Think*, 15-16.
[14]Smith, *Internet Is Not What You Think*, 37.

In describing this more profound form of attention, one that resists the pressures of monetized distraction, Smith uses the term "transformative moral commitment." This is a commitment to true attention, to the possibility of transformative encounter with the other. Smith suggests it is possible that the crisis of attention in our time is not an inevitable outcome of the interconnectivity and abundance of available information that characterizes the digital age. Rather, it is a result of economic forces and "the excessively narrow channeling of our cognitive and emotional investment down pathways that are structurally guaranteed to limit or prevent personal transformation."[15] This possibility raises the question of what potential there might be for positive transformation that occurs through the internet.

FROM ICLOUD TO I-THOU: RESISTING ALIENATION AND OBJECTIFICATION

As the invisibility of the internet developed, the attention economy gained momentum by burning the fuel of monetized distraction. We have accepted as normal the fragmentation of our minds by ever-present appeals for our focus and the diminishment of our mental and emotional resources. Smith proposes that shallow engagement—what he calls "bare observation without attention"—is incapable of effecting real change. Smith summarizes his concept of real attention by writing, "Attention opens up the attender to the object, so that it may as it were go to work on the individual, bringing that person into a changed state and thus exercising a power we ordinarily restrict to agent-others worthy of a second-person stance."[16] Smith's philosophy of transformative moral commitment resonates with the work of an earlier thinker: Austrian-Jewish philosopher Martin Buber.

Buber's best-known work, *I and Thou* (originally written in German in 1923 and translated to English in 1937), is built on the concept of two "primary words." These are stances the human being takes toward the world, thereby silently speaking about their own identity and the object of their attention: *I-Thou* or *I-It*. The I-Thou denotes a deep engagement that summons the whole self into relationship. The I-It describes shallow experience that uses

---

[15]Smith, *Internet Is Not What You Think*, 37.
[16]Smith, *Internet Is Not What You Think*, 27.

the world rather than being transformed by it. In Buber's words, "The primary word *I-Thou* can only be spoken with the whole being. The primary word *I-It* can never be spoken with the whole being." The stance a human person takes toward the world, either I-Thou or I-It, reshapes the *I* that is the person's own identity while also profoundly changing their engagement with the world: "As experience, the world belongs to the primary word *I-It*. The primary word *I-Thou* establishes the world of relation."[17]

As the human person interacts with the world on the level of I-It, they experience and *use* the world for the purpose of "the sustaining, relieving, and equipping of human life." As the world of *It* grows, direct experience is increasingly replaced with the indirect; knowledge is acquired and mastery is developed; and the spiritual life is shrouded and blocked off by a stance of transforming the world while refusing to allow the self to be transformed: "It is the obstacle; for the development of the ability to experience comes about mostly through the decrease of man's power to enter into relation—the power in virtue of which alone man can live the life of the spirit."[18] Shallow experience is found in the world of It; deep relation is encountered in the world of Thou.

We see how many of our experiences of the internet seem to turn the world into an object and alienate us from other people. We scroll through advertisements screaming for our attention, constantly repeating the refrains of materialism and consumerism. Even in our own social media profiles, we often self-objectify as we make use of ourselves for the sake of likes, shares, and comments. Here our self becomes the "It" in the I-It relationship, and we become disconnected both from ourselves and from others, who cannot be allowed to truly see us. We fall into spirals of dopamine-seeking performance and shame-induced comparison. I have experienced this many times, in subtle and overt ways. Our exploitation in the attention economy generates profit, but it does not generate holistic well-being or growth in Christian virtue.

But even on the internet, there is the potential for real connection. While I have experienced alienation online, I have also spent an hour with a mentor, a few friends, or a group of church members and felt genuine

---

[17]Martin Buber, *I and Thou* (New York: Scribner, 1958), 12-13.
[18]Buber, *I and Thou*, 35-36.

connection, true relationship, and transformative encouragement. How can this be?

Buber suggests that the spiritual life is dependent on the primary word *I-Thou*. Spiritual depth is not found in the depths of the self but in relation. We can live "in the spirit," in connection between I and Thou, by engaging with others and with the world with our whole being. While Buber writes of the necessity of the I-Thou stance, he also acknowledges that experience on the level of I-It is both inevitable and needed. Both are a part of the human condition. For Buber, the I-Thou is not a constant state of spiritual attunement with God, the world, or other people, but a capacity to enter into moments of profound meaning and relationship. Buber describes causality as the chain of events and experiences on the level of I-It. These experiences cannot be avoided, but the human person can move from I-It back into I-Thou and be transformed toward freedom. Buber describes a person who is "able to cross again and again the threshold of the holy place wherein he was not able to remain.... There, on the threshold, the response, the spirit, is kindled ever new within him; here, in an unholy and needy country, this spark is to be proved."[19]

While Smith emphasizes the challenges to true attention (transformative moral commitment, which is analogous to Buber's I-Thou) in the age of the internet, it is important to highlight that the challenge of shifting between shallow, disengaged experience that merely uses the world and deep, profound connection in relationship is not a new one. It has always been a part of the human condition.[20] The obstacles we face today are unprecedented and take novel forms, but the root problem has not changed. We all shift between I-Thou and I-It constantly through our lives, not only online.

Almost a century before Smith wrote his warning about the obstacles to true attention posed by the attention economy, Buber wrote of the impact of true relation. This posture creates "a world that is homely and houselike," which makes it possible for humanity to build safety, meaning, and relationship, to build "dwellings for God and dwellings for [people]," to "fill

---

[19]Buber, *I and Thou*, 36, 45.
[20]See Genesis 28:16, "Then Jacob woke from his sleep and said, 'Surely the LORD is in this place—and I did not know it!'" Spirituality writ large can be seen as the experience or pursuit of deep connection with reality that moves beyond distraction and shallow, transactional, or apathetic relation.

swaying time with new hymns and songs." In contrast, Buber speaks of the risk of a culture spiraling down into disconnection—if it does not remain "centred in the living and continually renewed relational event, then it hardens into the world of *It*."[21]

Human beings long for home. Humanity's desire for genuine connection with the world, other people, and, within a Christian framework, God, is fundamental. But when a home changes to become something unfamiliar, that sense of rootedness leading to flourishing life can be disrupted. In the internet, something new has arrived in the world and introduced unanticipated transformations. The challenge that faces us today is how we are to continue attending to the presence of God, other people, and ourselves in a world that is changing.

Even after his dire warnings about the potential of the internet and the attention economy to obstruct genuine transformation, Smith has a hopeful word to say about the internet:

> Although the Internet is the primary motor for the spread of this new system, it is very likely that whatever new sanctuaries we might yet hope to build, where the rapacious logic of this new system does not have any purchase, will *also* come through the Internet. . . . Remarkably, then, the Internet is simultaneously our greatest affliction and our greatest hope; the present situation is intolerable, but there is no going back. . . . The only solution to the problems the Internet has left us with is to shape the Internet, or at least certain corners of it, into something else.[22]

Our habitual means and structures have been shaken, and the ground is moving under our feet. We do not yet know what will emerge, but we have the opportunity and responsibility to build these shifting stones into "a house where love can dwell."[23]

EXPERT WITNESS: SCHOLARLY AND PRACTICAL PERSPECTIVES ON THE IMPACT OF THE INTERNET

The attention economy that arose with the internet and social media presents significant problems for Christian discipleship. It is crucial for worship

---

[21] Buber, *I and Thou*, 46.
[22] Smith, *Internet Is Not What You Think*, 51.
[23] Marty Haugen, "All Are Welcome" (Chicago: GIA Publications, 1994).

leaders and church music scholars to grapple with these cultural forces of distraction, alienation, and objectification. However, it is also necessary to acknowledge other practical ways that the technological revolution of the internet has affected and may continue to affect church music. Similar to the printing press, the radio, and the television, the internet has raised new questions and anxieties for the church, challenged social and theological norms, and collided with existing structures around church music. While scholarship around these questions is still forming, the experts interviewed for this research have valuable insights to offer from their work.

Heidi Campbell described in an interview how the shift to online worship resulting from the pandemic presented new challenges and questions for pastors and worship leaders, as well as various reactions within church cultures. Speaking of the difficulties faced by pastors, Campbell points out that pastors lacked the technical training to make informed decisions around online worship. Their education, in general, lacked both practical skills and the flexible, creative, problem-solving approach needed with new technologies and shifting environments. Campbell remarks that pastors had to "basically put aside the whole model [they were] used to and in many ways start over."[24]

Many leaders were thrust into an environment they were ill-equipped to navigate. This required quick adaptation and learning new skills, both of which cost a great deal of energy and time. Established systems and structures such as local churches and denominations do not easily adapt to massive change. Campbell highlights that, even given the difficulty, adapting to change is an essential question for religious organizations. One of the central questions for the church will be how it adapts to the transformations brought about by the internet. She notes that many churches resisted this change in the past but now are facing real questions about how a continuing decision to remain disengaged from online spaces might affect their potential reach and even the survival of their organizations and communities.[25]

Along this line of thinking, Campbell offers an insightful historical analysis of our current technocultural moment in comparison to the early

---

[24]Heidi A. Campbell, interview by author, Zoom, January 20, 2023.
[25]Campbell, interview.

reactions to the printing press. She notes that the Catholic Church was initially in favor of the printing press as a means of standardizing religious training and proselytizing. This positive regard for the technology did not last, however. When the Protestant Reformation began, the media ceased being a lever for control and stability and became a tool for disruption and change. Campbell points out, "People are okay with technology as long as that allows them to keep doing what they're doing. But the people who've been the most vocal, especially before the pandemic, against technology were the people that had a much more structure-based, system-based understanding of religion." Campbell compares current organizations' rejection of the internet with the way the Catholic Church for a time condemned the printing press (which was challenging the organization's authority) but eventually had to accept and use the technology. This transformation was necessary but did result in a shift toward decreased control and stability. Campbell suggests that the Covid-19 pandemic represented a similar moment for many churches:

> I think the pandemic was that moment when we're saying, okay, we have to embrace the technology and we have to be willing to give up some of our control, realizing . . . we're not experts in technology. It means it changes a little bit the shape of our service and whatnot. . . . So I think this is a great moment. . . . Are people going to roll with it or are they going to shrink back? . . . And I think we're seeing [in] churches, especially in 2022, going into 2023, that those two reactions are very pronounced.[26]

The internet is not an unalloyed good to be embraced wholeheartedly; however, we should also be aware that our structures of religious power and authority (regardless of denomination or tradition) will tend to bring their theological authority to bear in ways that defend their own interests and stability.

While church leaders generally struggled to adapt to the online environment, shifting worship online also raised difficult questions for worship leaders in particular. Campbell notes that this change brought up questions about the purpose of musical worship. She notes that many people described musical worship as a community event, to gather the people together.

---

[26] Campbell, interview.

Thus, anxieties arose about whether an online mediation of musical worship could be a genuine expression of communal gathering: "And so the fear was, well, if we just put our people up on the screen, and there's nobody in the congregation, it's just a performance. . . . How do we place those people on a screen so it actually encourages community?"[27]

Campbell also notes that these efforts to cultivate community through online music revealed for some churches that their musical practices were not as communal as they had assumed. She says, "A lot of churches . . . either didn't want to realize . . . or they tried to ignore that we thought we were building communities through our worship . . . but actually, it's just a performance." The task of presenting services online highlighted these concerns and questions, inviting self-examination and critique of habitual approaches.[28]

The sudden broad adoption of online worship, then, introduced new struggles for ministers due to a lack of skills using the new technologies, while also bringing into question the legitimacy of previously accepted patterns of practice. When a new variable changes our media ecology, we are likely to experience both responses: a difficulty adapting and an awareness of the imperfections of our existing and familiar methods.

One practical example of the challenge to adapt arose around issues of copyright. Just as the printing press presented new possibilities for sharing music, leading to the need for musicians to protect their work, the internet allows for widespread sharing of content, including that created by artists. Copyright is a much more developed system at the time of this writing, and many churches struggled to navigate that system while making the shift online. Campbell points out how churches needed to address questions of how to appropriately display licensing information for music on their streaming services, and whether portions of their videos on platforms such as YouTube would be flagged as copyright infringement or have the audio silenced. Campbell describes churches that felt blindsided by this shift: "This is something we've never had to think about when we're now in multiple spaces. We know the rules *here* [in physical church], but what are the rules in the digital world? How might that change?"[29]

---

[27]Campbell, interview.
[28]Campbell, interview.
[29]Campbell, interview.

Understanding this set of issues was not a struggle only for individual congregations, however. Joe Iovino of United Methodist Communications was involved in denomination-level efforts to provide online worship resources for United Methodist churches and encountered similar barriers. Copyright was a major obstacle for the denomination, as it was not readily apparent what the organization could legally do to provide resources and connect with local congregations. United Methodist Communications hoped to broadcast services for the denomination, but copyright restricted their efforts to produce their own worship service or digitally host a local church's service. The communications agency was not equipped with the proper licenses for these kinds of projects because they had not been necessary in a prepandemic world.[30] Even an established denomination such as the United Methodist Church struggled to find ways to move forward in the new media environment.

Apart from copyright issues, congregations were also wrestling with what a meaningful online offering might look like. Taylor Burton-Edwards recounts the shortcomings of much of what occurred on early pandemic worship livestreams. Burton-Edwards remarks, "Just a documentation by video of what's going on in the room does not constitute effective online worship practice at this point." While many churches have been obtaining equipment and learning more about how to produce a more appealing visual offering, most online worship services still seem lacking in terms of genuine participation. Burton-Edwards recounts that a church where he served started by "literally taking somebody's cell phone camera, mounting it somewhere and streaming that to Facebook."[31] A similar practice happened in my own previous church for a time. This is understandable, given the sudden and huge change brought about by the pandemic lockdown. However, the tendency to simply provide video feed of a typical Sunday service falls short of allowing for meaningful engagement and formation. Allison Norton draws on her research of congregations across the United States to comment on this dynamic:

> One of the things that we see is many churches, especially smaller and midsized churches, are doing what could be called hybrid, but they're simply livestreaming what happens in a face-to-face setting. And that has a lot of

---

[30]Joe Iovino, interview by author, Zoom, January 23, 2023.
[31]Taylor Burton-Edwards, interview by author, Zoom, January 25, 2023.

limitations, a lot of questions around... what involvement is happening? How are you facilitating a sense of belonging to the larger community in this group?[32]

Norton's reflection raises the question of what would be required for online worship to facilitate meaningful involvement and belonging in community. It is possible to conceive of the answer in terms of high production-value streaming such as services produced by megachurches. However, this ideal (if it is indeed ideal) is not feasible for most churches. Burton-Edwards combines demographic knowledge with personal experience to make a compelling case. He emphasizes, "The vast majority of congregations are fewer than one hundred in average worship attendance.... Those congregations simply don't have the capacity to do this." Personnel, technology, and equipment are all major issues, leading Burton-Edwards to conclude, "Nothing about a church that size, which is the vast majority of American congregations [Burton-Edwards estimates over 72 percent], makes it a reasonable candidate for livestreaming." Burton-Edwards recounts his experience as a pastor during the pandemic:

> Well, during the pandemic, everybody needed to do something like [online worship]. But I can tell you as a working pastor during the pandemic that for a small church, this was an impossible burden because I was the only person who could do it. And I had to do the whole thing myself. Zoom did not work for my people. And trying to do any other format did not work for my people. The only thing that began to work for my people was for me to produce a videotaped worship service every week, which was taking fourteen hours for twenty-eight minutes of a service, minus the sermon prep. This is unsustainable.[33]

Burton-Edwards also highlights a demographic issue. A research group called Faith Communities Today began tracking congregational demographic trends in 2000 and published a report in 2020. According to this report, while 70 percent of congregations are smaller than 100, 70 percent of American Christians attend churches larger than 250 (these churches represent 4 percent of American congregations).[34] The online church streaming

---

[32] Allison Norton, interview by author, Zoom, February 23, 2023.
[33] Burton-Edwards, interview.
[34] "FACT 2020 Survey Results," *Faith Communities Today*, October 25, 2019, https://faithcommunities today.org/fact-2020-survey/.

space is dominated by large churches, which set the norms for what online worship "should" be. This connects back to Campbell's remarks about new expectations being placed on church leaders. Pastors and ministers have not been trained to be video editors and online entrepreneurs. But as Burton-Edwards points out, the pandemic and surrounding technological changes and cultural expectations pressured churches to compete in a market dominated by atypical congregations. This raises a crucial question for churches in a postpandemic era: How can these communities be sustainable in this new landscape?[35]

Sustainability for worshiping communities will be a major concern going forward. Campbell reflects somberly on the prognosis for many local congregations in the new environment:

> I believe in the next twenty years we're going to see a large portion of churches dying. And my fear is the churches that will die will be the kind of small, especially mainline denominations, the ones that kind of [say] . . . we have this tradition and we're so grounded in the tradition. We're not looking at how we might adapt. And a lot of times people say, "Oh, if we change the liturgy, then we've changed the culture, we've changed our faith." You can innovate liturgy, you can innovate practices, and not throw out your theology, but it does mean some negotiation. So I believe the churches that will survive are the ones that are able to innovate and work within those kind of structures. The ones that are going to die are the ones that are not willing to, especially with older congregation members that are very resistant to—and I say it's technology; it's just one of the markers of that resistance rather than the main thing.[36]

Campbell takes no delight in acknowledging the likely trajectory of these smaller congregations in America. Additionally, she acknowledges where she sees the trends in more digitally mediated worship moving, noting the likely outcome of more multisite church networks resourced by megachurches. Campbell expresses concern that "worship entertainment" will become more widespread and wonders, "What kind of a theology is going to be prevalent because it sells well? How will that affect Christian culture?"[37] It is possible that these expressions of worship will become more prevalent; however, it is

---

[35]Burton-Edwards, interview.
[36]Campbell, interview.
[37]Campbell, interview.

not a foregone conclusion, and the church as a worshiping community may take many forms as we move into the future.

Continuing in the register of large-scale religious trends in America, Campbell notes that the changes she is tracing have been occurring for the past hundred years. However, the invention and application of new digital technologies, and especially the forced move online brought about by the Covid-19 pandemic, accelerated the changes into "hyperdrive."[38] When asked what changes would most likely affect music ministries, Campbell referenced multisite reality (mentioned briefly above) and convergent practice, which I will expand on here. Campbell states,

> Convergent practice is the idea that people feel that their spirituality isn't just coming from one source. They pick and mix. And this is really true. You may go to a church that is all hymn based, but you may listen to the KSBJ or whatever the big contemporary station is, and so . . . the technology allows [people] to draw from these multiple sources. . . . So this kind of picking, mixing from your tradition and other spaces has become common. And the Internet didn't start this. It just made it easier.[39]

The trend of convergent practice has been growing for decades. However, it is likely that it will grow even more with the normalization of online technologies permeating culture. Convergent practice goes well beyond expressions such as the radio and can include other media such as podcasts, YouTube channels, or blogs, as well as physical gatherings that take place outside a typical church building.

Combining with convergent practice, a major demographic shift is also approaching. Campbell references the research of groups such as Pew and Barna that report the increasing number of religious "nones," who are not affiliated with any particular religious tradition but experience their spirituality through a do-it-yourself approach. In addition to the nones, Campbell notes the increase of the "dones"—people who, especially in the past few years, have lost the desire to engage with the institutional church. Campbell depicts the dones as people who self-describe as Christian and may identify with a particular denominational flavor or theology but "have no affiliation

---

[38]Campbell, interview.
[39]Campbell, interview.

and have no desire to go to the church regularly. . . . They basically are done with church." Campbell cites a Pew Research projection that "within thirty to fifty years the US will no longer be a Christian majority nation."[40]

Campbell believes this ongoing demographic shift will have huge implications for churches broadly, as well as more specifically for the structures and expressions of church music. She points to the Christian music industry, which has developed a structure around what has been considered a viable market, culture, and community. That industry may look very different in a future when Christianity's role in American society has changed: "If you are no longer the main power brokers and your cultural capital is shifted or diminished, that's a real identity shift as well as a practice shift that has to take place."[41]

There are shifts happening in our churches and in the world around us that are beyond our control. There are also ways we can learn to create practices and communal patterns that are simultaneously meaningful and adaptable, rooted in tradition and flexible enough to survive a new environment. We can resonate with the words of 1 John 3:2: "Beloved, we are God's children now; what we will be has not yet been revealed." We do not know what kinds of transformations, deaths, or resurrections we may undergo.

One potential transformation lies in the direction of metaverse or blended-reality church.[42] Virtual reality pastor DJ Soto projects a somewhat different future for Christian communities, claiming, "In five to ten years, the future of the church will be the metaverse." Soto clarifies that this does not mean that digital technology will replace the physical church but rather that digital space will be the central location and starting point for connections and interactions, which will then lead (in many cases) to proximal interactions and events: "Whether it's a Sunday morning, one-hour event, [or] a Bible study, it's all going to be based out of your centralized metaverse." Soto suggests that this should not strike us as strange, because even today many people connect

---

[40]Campbell, interview. See Reem Nadeem, "2. Projecting U.S. Religious Groups' Population Shares by 2070," Pew Research Center, September 13, 2022, https://www.pewresearch.org/religion/2022/09/13/projecting-u-s-religious-groups-population-shares-by-2070/.
[41]Campbell, interview.
[42]This can be understood as an extension of a church's online presence, involving virtual reality spaces, which users might inhabit and engage with through a variety of technologies, whether virtual reality headsets, smartphones, or computers.

first with a church through a website or social media account and enter a physical building only after multiple online interactions. According to Soto, the changes brought about by this technological revolution and accelerated by the pandemic will lead to virtual, online spaces being a central starting point for many churches, playing a similar role to what a church website does today.[43]

Churches may not take only one form in the coming decades. It is quite possible for multiple differing expressions of faith communities to exist and even flourish. However, it seems likely that the landscape will change significantly, and our musical worship practices will need to shift as well.

CHRISTIAN FORMATION AND CHURCH MUSIC IN THE AGE OF THE INTERNET

At this point, the concepts described above—the ubiquitous presence of the internet, the attention economy and its obstacles to true attention, the importance of transformative moral commitment or the I-Thou stance, and the challenges churches face in adapting to the internet—need to be brought to bear in relation to church music. This framework of concepts is important in that it directs the ways in which we can imagine a future for the church's music. It suggests that our interest should not be in how the church can produce streamed events that have high viewer retention rate and boast impressive production value to enter into the economic battleground for human attention. This kind of jockeying for position in the attention economy is unlikely to be successful, except for a small minority of highly resourced churches. Even in cases where attention seeking is successful in economic terms, it is questionable whether it is theologically consistent with Christ's call to the church.

My claim is parallel to retrospective theological critiques of the church-growth movement. In a book review of David Goodhew's 2015 edited volume *Towards a Theology of Church Growth*, Martyn Percy writes about the "homogenous unit principle" that theorized people would more easily join and contribute to the growth of churches made up of people like themselves. Percy assesses this approach theologically, saying, "In America, it is always

---

[43] DJ Soto, interview by author, Zoom, January 13, 2023.

hard to say where business ends and religion begins. The two are not so much joined at the hip as genetically spliced together." He goes on to claim that placing hope in people self-sorting into like-minded groups, while it might be an effective business strategy, is an ecclesiological disaster and makes numerical growth a "fetish or apotheosis" while actually running counter to what Percy describes as "the deeper political and cultural demands of the Kingdom of God." Percy calls for believers to remember that "the Church of Jesus Christ—like the ministry of Jesus—was radically inclusive, and supra-tribal from the outset. Faithfulness was always championed before indices of numerical success."[44]

In an attention economy that provides metrics of viewer counts, click-through rates, and likes or reactions, the church will be tempted toward these kinds of numerical criteria once again. But Percy contends, "Jesus was seldom interested in *quantity*; the Kingdom is about small numbers and rich quality. Yet we live in a culture that is obsessed by measuring things numerically, and judging success from this."[45] Reaching countless people online in ways that do not invite transformative moral commitment, or true attention to the deep reality of God's presence in creation, is a fool's errand.

While Christian formation can occur through digitally mediated means, it must intentionally step outside the dominant narratives of the attention economy. Rather than applying the methods or ideology of the church-growth movement to the internet, we should consider that the church is called to resist the demands of the attention economy, while making effective and faithful use of the tools at our disposal. Even two millennia before the internet, Jesus did not fight for people's attention but taught and ministered in ways that bewildered and even drove away many people, operating outside the economic and political systems of even his time. His ministry was thus antithetical to the ideals of the attention economy. Social media platforms may be responsible to shareholders to grow, and therefore must colonize human attention; Christ's church, however, is responsible to God, and its growth is a result of the Holy Spirit animating the body of Christ.

---

[44] Martyn Percy, Review of *Towards a Theology of Church Growth*, edited by David Goodhew, *Ecclesiology* 13, no. 1 (January 2017): 136.
[45] Percy, Review of *Towards a Theology*, 136.

The questions most important for scholars and leaders of church music are these: Can church music in online worship play a role in this transformation? How can digital uses of church music avoid the pitfalls of the attention economy and facilitate moral commitment and meaningful engagement? The answers we reach must avoid two less helpful extremes. People located at the first extreme might ask, "How do we compete for people's attention in an online space of never-ending, monetized distraction? How can we increase production value to stop them clicking away? How do we generate more views?" These concerns are not entirely insignificant but miss the main point. Those occupying the opposite extreme might say, "The way we present worship online does not matter—just stick a phone camera in front of our typical Sunday service, and the real believers will come." This kind of ineffective and unreflective use of a new medium does not constitute faithful stewardship.

Instead, what might it look like to cultivate spaces on the internet characterized by transformative moral commitment rather than spectacle-driven distraction? How can we encourage I-Thou relation with God and others in a world dominated by I-It objectification? If this is our goal, what might faithful, creative, transformative use of online media for ministry look like? How might we think more deeply about the church's music in our current technological revolution as our experience and practice are in flux?

To address these questions, further theological and theoretical work remains to be done to deepen and nuance our reflection about music's use in worship in a digitally mediated age. Much of what has happened since the Covid-19 pandemic has been stopgap, pragmatic choices made of necessity. This is not necessarily a problem; what is concerning is that much of the broader conversation in the church about online worship has been shallow and unreflective. In the following chapters, I will bring interdisciplinary perspectives and more thorough philosophical and theological thought to this important question: How do we love God and neighbor through church music in the age of the internet and social media?

Activity and Embodiment

Almost everything that we think of as dichotomous is in fact spectral.

JOHN GREEN

THE RAPID CHANGE BROUGHT ABOUT by the Covid-19 pandemic highlighted and intensified conversations about our bodily presence and participation in worship. At my own church, things that had long been assumed were thrown into doubt: could we gather in physical space safely, and what precautions ought we to take? How would our relationships and communities be impacted by this crisis? If we offered online spaces for worship, could meaningful Christian formation take place? Our own bodies, and the bodies of our congregants, became the focus of attention in unfamiliar ways.

A new awareness of our shared embodiment came with unanticipated and legitimate anxieties and fears. To a very real extent, our bodies became a danger to each other, and we did not yet know if our habitual shared activities were safe or might put vulnerable people in our community at risk. This moment called for theological triage, and we had to spring into action to care for our congregants' bodies and souls. The same was true in local churches and religious organizations across the world. At least early on, it seemed that

---

Vlogbrothers, "Planets Don't Exist," October 7, 2022, video, 13:59, www.youtube.com/watch?v=S2L0sWMEG-A&t=621s.

our embodied activity together went from being a given to potentially being taken away. We were experiencing what felt like a complete 180° turn overnight; our church was no longer full, but empty.

LOST IN THE ONES AND ZEROS: UNHELPFUL BINARIES ABOUT ONLINE INTERACTIONS

One of the many challenges of understanding worship during a pandemic and in the early stages of a technological revolution has been the difficulty of making sense of change and new experiences. A consistent way human beings strive to create order out of our chaotic experience is by separating people, objects, practices, and ideas into binaries: us and them, in and out, good and evil. Creating binaries is in one sense a necessary and potentially positive coping strategy to deal with the complexities of life. We cannot afford to be paralyzed by indecision; therefore, we simplify or caricature reality to fit more neatly into categories we can easily manipulate and implement to solve problems. In another sense, however, this tendency limits our capacities to think creatively, appreciate nuance, and find new solutions. This limiting tendency can be seen in our categories around online and hybrid religious practices.

In this and the following chapter, I will endeavor to reframe four dichotomies in ways that are both more realistic and more productive. These include black-and-white categorizations of practices and experiences as either active or passive, as embodied or disembodied, as unmediated or mediated, and as real or virtual. In conversations around online worship since the pandemic began, popular assumptions and rhetoric have sometimes followed this logic: worship should be active, embodied, unmediated, and real; but online interactions are passive, disembodied, mediated, and virtual; therefore, digitally mediated worship practices and communities are illegitimate and will be ineffective.

While it is pervasive, this logic ultimately fails to be convincing because it does not adequately reflect lived experience. In what follows I will explore each category within these binaries with more nuance, in dialogue with recent interdisciplinary scholarship, and thereby problematize the dichotomies that have been built up around them. It is necessary to name, acknowledge, and meaningfully grapple with each of these before constructing a productive theology of worship using online media.

THE FIRST BINARY: ACTIVE VERSUS PASSIVE

> Mother Church earnestly desires that all the faithful should be led to that fully conscious, and active participation in liturgical celebrations which is demanded by the very nature of the liturgy. Such participation by the Christian people as "a chosen race, a royal priesthood, a holy nation, a redeemed people (1 Pet. 2:9; cf. 2:4-5), is their right and duty by reason of their baptism.[1]

These words are from *Sacrosanctum Concilium*, one of the constitutions of Vatican II. Written in 1963, they represent a commitment within the Catholic Church to correct for an outsized emphasis on what might be termed presentational liturgical elements performed by clergy, as well as to facilitate greater engagement by the congregation in worship. Within Catholicism, "fully conscious and active participation" became a high value, guiding decisions made about liturgy.

Similar ideas and priorities have appeared in Protestant spaces. For example, *Christianity Today* published an article on March 17, 2020, titled, "How to Lead Online Worship Without Losing Your Soul—or Body." Fuller Theological Seminary professor W. David O. Taylor makes several suggestions for pastors and worship leaders navigating new circumstances at the beginning of the pandemic, including the following: "If our aim is to foster the full, conscious, and active participation of the laity in worship, then we should look for ways to get people actively, rather than passively, involved. How do we counter the spectator mode that sitting in front of a screen may engender in us? Get the body moving!"[2] Even in this popular-level article targeted to Protestant audiences, the language of *Sacrosanctum Concilium* about participation appears as a primary goal of worship leadership.[3]

Regardless of denomination, ministers and churches often place a heavy emphasis on active participation in conversations around the church's music. For worship leaders, the degree of engagement and active participation of congregants is a major gauge of how effectively they are ministering. In churches of

---

[1] Pope Paul VI, *Sacrosanctum Concilium*, December 4, 1963, www.vatican.va/archive/hist_councils/ii_vatican_council/documents/vat-ii_const_19631204_sacrosanctum-concilium_en.html.
[2] W. David O. Taylor, "How to Lead Online Worship Without Losing Your Soul—or Body," *Christianity Today*, March 17, 2020, www.christianitytoday.com/pastors/2020/march-web-exclusives/how-to-lead-online-worship-without-losing-your-soul-or-body.html.
[3] For discussion of this crossover from a Catholic perspective, see Anthony Ruff, "After Vatican II: Are We All Protestants Now? Or Are We All Catholics Now?," *The Hymn* 64, no. 1 (Winter 2013): 6-12.

varying size, the practical contours of individual music ministries will diverge widely. The resources and personnel available, the particular skills of volunteers at a given church, and the musical history and identity of the local church will hugely influence the music made there. However, in whatever context, facilitating the active participation of the people seems to be a positive and (hopefully) attainable goal. The congregants' active response and engagement becomes the litmus test for whether music in worship is "working." In her book *Singing the Congregation*, Monique Ingalls describes this dynamic in the context of worship concerts, which are constructed around the value of participation.

> In order to be "authentic worship," the worship concert must be experienced as a participatory performance, in which the boundary between the worship leader at center stage and the audience in the stadium seats is collapsed because both are engaged in the act of worship. Attendees must understand both themselves and the worship leaders onstage as "worshipers"—equal participants in the activity of worship. They do so by emphasizing participatory qualities and values and distancing themselves from the social roles and the goals of presentational performance.[4]

While placing a high value on active participation might at first seem like a commonsense conclusion, within our present context of navigating and negotiating new expressions of church in the wake of the Covid-19 pandemic and accelerating technocultural change, it requires further examination.

Popular conversation regarding digitally mediated expressions of church often perceives online interactions as passive rather than active. A July 29, 2020, blog post on the website The Network: Christian Reformed Church articulated a refrain often heard during the pandemic. Theodore Lim writes, "I deeply worry that online worship will be reduced to passive worship rather than active worship through the participation of worshipers."[5] This kind of anxiety, while not wholly unfounded, can lead to an instinctive, even prereflective, bias against practices that are mediated by new technological forms. Digital practices are commonly categorized as passive and therefore perceived as unsuited to worship.

---

[4] Monique Marie Ingalls, *Singing the Congregation: How Contemporary Worship Music Forms Evangelical Community* (New York: Oxford University Press, 2018), 56.

[5] "Is Online Worship as Good as It Seems?," The Network: Christian Reformed Church, July 29, 2020, https://network.crcna.org/topic/worship/general-worship/online-worship-good-it-seems.

I suggest that the high valuation of active participation, and dismissal of practices that seem passive, represents an overcorrection. While some historic practices of the church arguably swung to an extreme of passivity and a lack of participation by the people, the solution is not necessarily to swing to the opposite extreme of always requiring maximum activity from believers. Faith has always included both active and passive aspects. In what follows, I will introduce philosophical and theological perspectives relevant to active or passive participation in music. Robert Pfaller's work on interpassivity will provide a useful category for understanding worship practices, and scholars who engage with interpassivity in areas related to digital media, music, philosophy, and theology will provide additional insights.

I will also examine the assumption that worship is primarily an active process, both theologically and practically. There is good biblical grounding for a theology of worship that finds a balance between activity and passivity; further, in practical terms we already live in this balance, even if our instinct is to disavow it. My goal is to point out and refute the tendency within conversations around worship to perceive active and passive participation as dichotomous categories that carry predetermined value judgments. Examining this presumed dichotomy with more nuance will provide opportunity to reexamine the decisions we make in worship and open space to imagine what meaningful active and passive engagement with digital technologies might look like within the church's communal life.

INTERPASSIVITY: AN INTRODUCTION

My starting point for troubling the active/passive dichotomy is the idea of interpassivity. Robert Pfaller has been a major proponent of interpassivity as a useful framework. At the opening of his 2017 book *Interpassivity: The Aesthetics of Delegated Enjoyment*, he describes how delegating *work* to others is a common feature of our society.[6] Pfaller goes on to attempt an explanation for confusing dynamics that seem to involve, rather than a delegation of *work*, a delegation of *consumption* or *enjoyment*:

---

[6] Robert Pfaller, *Interpassivity: The Aesthetics of Delegated Enjoyment* (Edinburgh: Edinburgh University Press, 2017), chapter 1, Kindle.

Activity and Embodiment

Rather than delegating, for instance, their responsibilities to representative agents, interpassive people delegate precisely those things that they *enjoy* doing—those things that they do for pleasure, out of passion or conviction. Rather than letting others *work* for them, they let them *enjoy* for them. In other words, they delegate *passivity* to others rather than *activity*.[7]

Pfaller describes interpassivity as "a pleasant consuming attitude . . . a 'passivity,'" and says, "The *enjoyment* of something is—partly or even totally—delegated to other people or to a technical device."[8]

Pfaller's motivation for developing the idea of interpassivity is partly a reaction against "the assumption that 'activity' is fundamentally good." For instance, Pfaller describes art exhibits that prioritize interactive installations and takes issue with the assumption that "activating the beholder will always be aesthetically productive and politically satisfying." Instead, Pfaller claims, "Becoming an active subject cannot be turned into any universal political solution. Thinking about interpassivity therefore means no less than investigating a basic, unquestioned assumption of most emancipatory movements since 1968, namely the assumption that active is better than passive." Interactive art requires observers "to contribute creative 'activity' for the completion of the artwork. The interactive artwork is a work that is not yet finished, but that 'waits' for some creative work that has to be added to it by the observer."[9]

Pfaller cites an example from philosopher Slavoj Žižek, who proposes the use of canned laughter in comedic television shows as an instance of interpassive art. The show laughs at itself, and so the viewer is relieved of the duty to laugh outwardly to express their inward amusement. A similar dynamic can be seen in video game streams, such as on the popular online platform Twitch.tv. On this platform, video gamers stream themselves playing a game to an audience, who watches while interacting with the streamer and other audience members via chat.

The spectrum of activity and passivity can also be experienced musically. While some music listeners may occasionally choose to apply their full attention and focus to listening intentionally to the details of a recording or

---

[7] Pfaller, *Interpassivity*, introduction.
[8] Pfaller, *Interpassivity*, chapter 1.
[9] Pfaller, *Interpassivity*, introduction, chapter 3.

performance, most people listen to music more passively most of the time. Anahid Kassabian's book *Ubiquitous Listening: Affect, Attention, and Distributed Subjectivity* discusses this dynamic. Kassabian claims that "*ubiquitous musics*" fill our waking hours without calling for focused attention, or "active listening," but nonetheless produce affective and bodily responses. Music literally and figuratively *moves* us, whether our engagement with it is active or passive.[10] Music does not affect our bodies and emotions only when we are fully, actively, and consciously engaged with it; rather, music infuses most of our lived experience, regardless of how active or passive we are. The spectrum of these experiences, from active to passive, may have different impacts, but that full range of experience is worth considering.

Anecdotally, during the height of the Covid-19 pandemic and the accompanying disruption and lockdown, I found myself seeking out interpassive forms of entertainment, including video game streams and music. Like many others, I was coping with the stress of an extended crisis, the difficulty of continuing to be productive in the midst of change and Zoom fatigue (I will discuss Zoom fatigue in more depth later). By the end of the day I felt I lacked the energy to even enjoy a hobby such as playing video games, making music, or even listening attentively to music. The opportunity to interpassively delegate that enjoyment to someone else provided me a space to relax that felt otherwise inaccessible.

A THEOLOGY OF INTERPASSIVITY

But can interpassivity, used frequently to apply to entertainment, be legitimately applied to religion? Intriguingly, Pfaller suggests that interpassivity may be a useful theoretical tool for understanding rituals, including religious rituals: "Through rituals, individuals delegate their religious beliefs to interpassive media [meaning the person or technology to which they delegate consumption]. Not only is interpassivity based on ritual, but the ritual itself is based on interpassivity."[11]

Carolyn J. Mackie applies the category of interpassivity to Christian faith in intriguing ways. She first draws on Žižek's example of someone on vacation

---

[10]Anahid Kassabian, *Ubiquitous Listening: Affect, Attention, and Distributed Subjectivity* (Berkeley: University of California Press, 2013), xi. Emphasis original.
[11]Pfaller, *Interpassivity*, chapter 3.

Activity and Embodiment 53

feeling a compulsion to enjoy themselves, so much so that their guilt or anxiety about not enjoying the vacation enough actually sabotages that enjoyment. This guilt or anxiety to enjoy is described as a "monstrous duty," and relief from it is framed as a "liberating potential." Mackie picks up the language of "monstrous duty" and applies it to interpassivity in religious practice:

> Who has not felt this "monstrous duty" to enjoy, to sorrow, etc.—or the "liberating potential" of being relieved of this duty? Perhaps . . . interpassive displacement . . . may carry . . . potential to create a space in which I can feel and believe more authentically. And perhaps religious interpassive displacement can offer the opportunity for authentic faith and authentic emotional response to emerge.[12]

The "monstrous duty" is experienced interiorly by the individual; the solution is a displacement from the individual to rituals and communities that provide relief from the compulsion to produce piety and offer space to receive grace. As interpassivity can refer to delegation of enjoyment or consumption, it also can refer to the delegation or sharing of belief:

> The mode of encounter that we designate as belief is formulated in this communally constructed sphere. Perhaps Christian communities (and religious communities more generally) in their essence can be seen as fulfilling the function of providing others who will believe for me. When I am incapable of believing on my own, I can rest in the faith of others in my community. Indeed, perhaps we could go so far as to claim, as Žižek does, that belief always occurs through another. Perhaps the notion that I can believe entirely on my own is not only unthinkable but hubristic.[13]

If belief is itself something of an interpassive relationship, questions arise about the centrality of active participation on the individual level. The saving action of God through Christ's incarnation, ministry, death, resurrection, and ascension is worthy of response; in the words of an old hymn, "Love so amazing, so divine demands my soul, my life, my all."[14]

This "monstrous duty" for Christians to give their all during worship is attested to by scholars such as Joshua Busman and Monique Ingalls. In

---

[12]Carolyn J. Mackie, "Believing for Me: Žižek, Interpassivity, and Christian Experience" (paper presented at Institute for Christian Studies, May 2, 2013), 12.
[13]Mackie, "Believing for Me," 13.
[14]Isaac Watts, "When I Survey the Wondrous Cross" (1707).

describing an example from the Passion worship conference in which Louie Giglio called for the gathered congregation/concert audience to vocalize together, Busman points out that this kind of invitation or pressure (it could be experienced as either) from worship leaders is commonplace in a variety of worship contexts influenced by evangelical subculture. Congregations or "fan-worshipers" are asked to "lift up a shout . . . to perform and experience their own individual levels of spiritual sincerity." Busman suggests, "The enthusiasm with which one shouts is a direct reflection of God's might in that particular moment."[15] A worshiper in this kind of space is asked to "show up" for God, to embody how great God is by the intensity of their response. Their own sincerity is signaled and expressed by how loudly they shout or sing and how passionately they present their physicality to those around them. The worship environment simultaneously normalizes and demands this kind of worship from those present.

Ingalls also describes a similar dynamic in which the activity of gathered worshipers is essential to the intelligibility of the worship concert *as* worship. Worship leaders in these settings constantly exhort the crowds present to sing and take moments during the concert to highlight the sound of the congregation's collective voice: "All of these performative actions serve to mark the activity as 'worship' and reinforce the sense that concert audience members are full participants."[16] The spiritual stakes here are high; if the gathered worshipers as a group do not sufficiently participate in ways that signal their sincerity and the presence of God, the legitimacy of the entire event comes into question. This also occurs on the individual level. If a particular person within the crowd of passionate worshipers either fails to embody this intensity or fails to feel the emotions appropriate to their external actions, the inward legitimacy of their own spirituality may be jeopardized.

Ingalls recounts an example of the burden of participation felt by a participant in the Passion conference. This worshiper desired to experience "genuine worship" with its requisite powerful emotions but also named feelings of exhaustion and disconnection due to the frequency and intensity of these worship concerts/services. In these moments of fatigue, this worship

---

[15]Joshua Kalin Busman, "(Re)Sounding Passion: Listening to American Evangelical Worship Music, 1997–2015" (PhD diss., University of North Carolina at Chapel Hill, 2015), 110.
[16]Ingalls, *Singing the Congregation*, 57.

concert-goer felt she was "just going through the motions because everyone around me was worshipping."[17] These worship concerts/services demanded a high burden of production from attendees, both to legitimate the spiritual significance of the event as worship and to validate each individual participant's identity as a worshiper.

But who among us can fully embody this commitment and fulfill the "monstrous duty" at all times? And is an anxiety or guilt about duty unfulfilled really God's desire for believers and the church? Rather than attempting to summon or manufacture pious affect or theological certainty within ourselves, we might do better to acknowledge that all our beliefs include an element of reliance on others, on a community that believes with and for us, and even on God, who believes with and for us: "Perhaps we could say that in this way, too, I believe through the other—through the divine Other in whom I believe."[18]

Mackie goes on to suggest a dynamic of also "worshiping through another." This features interpassive aspects to Christian experience and worship that provide space for worshipers to respond to God. Christian practices such as prayer, singing, and sacraments can become interpassive rituals, allowing for the delegation of enjoyment and belief to others who share our faith. As Mackie describes it, "I am relieved of the 'monstrous duty'" because "my experience is constituted by others." The surrounding community provides the words and expression of faith through communal prayer and singing: "If I find myself incapable of praying, singing, or speaking, the words do not for that reason cease to be spoken. I am carried by others (and I, in turn, carry them) through worship. I may be unable to laugh or cry, but I can rest in the knowledge that the Other is laughing and crying for me."[19]

Mackie's description mirrors Randall Bradley's discussion of the communal sharing inherent in corporate worship. In *From Memory to Imagination: Reforming the Church's Music*, Bradley touches on themes that are highly resonant with this discussion of interpassivity. When we as individuals cannot sing, praise, or pray, we rely on the support of the faith community to

---

[17] Monique Marie Ingalls, "Awesome in This Place: Sound, Space, and Identity in Contemporary North American Evangelical Worship" (PhD diss., University of Pennsylvania, 2008), 282.
[18] Mackie, "Believing for Me," 14.
[19] Mackie, "Believing for Me," 14.

carry our worship to God. Bradley describes "surrogate worship" as a "sacred task," in which members of the church act as priests for one another.[20] The broader dynamic of sharing with and relying on the worshiping community also reflects Paul's exhortation to the Galatian church: "Bear one another's burdens, and in this way you will fulfill the law of Christ" (Galatians 6:2).

Mackie continues by focusing on the Eucharist, which she calls "perhaps the ultimate expression of interpassivity in Christian worship." The sacrament involves a double displacement, resonating with the displacement of interpassivity; Christ's body and blood were given for us, and in celebrating the Eucharist we receive that gift. This transforms the "radically subjective displaced experience of Jesus Christ's death for me" into an "objectified" ritual displaced onto the communion elements. This interpassive ritual relieves the pressure from the worshiper to produce an appropriate subjective response to God's grace. The appropriate response has already been provided.[21]

This example of the Eucharist leads Mackie to suggest that the binary between activity and passivity is unhelpful, and in fact both are necessary elements of faith. Mackie wonders whether "perhaps authentic action can be undertaken only when counterbalanced by authentic passivity. And perhaps authentic passivity is possible only when a 'breathing space' has first been formed through interpassive means." Others Christians believing, worshiping, weeping, and rejoicing on our behalf becomes, in Mackie's view, "a means of grace."[22]

A passive God? Building on Mackie's theological description of interpassivity, there is scriptural and theological warrant for considering interpassivity a valid and important aspect of faith. Our cultural bias toward action might lead us to believe God is active, not passive. We might question how a passive God could save us. However, both activity and passivity are essential parts of God's faithful saving work in the world and of our own faithful response. If God's action is necessary, then God's passion is as well—the shared etymology of *passive* and *passion* (both from the Latin *pati*, meaning "to suffer") highlights this connection. Christ's passion is a central event of

---

[20] C. Randall Bradley, *From Memory to Imagination: Reforming the Church's Music* (Grand Rapids, MI: Eerdmans, 2012), 124.
[21] Mackie, "Believing for Me," 14-15.
[22] Mackie, "Believing for Me," 16.

Activity and Embodiment

salvation history; the passivity of God, being subject to the agency of and suffering the violence of humanity, cannot be ignored. Our hope in Christ as both priest (Hebrews 2:17) and sacrifice (Romans 3:25) requires both the displacement and delegation of our faith and the passivity of the Savior himself.

Even Pfaller's earlier description of art is applicable here. If interactive artwork requires completion by the observer, Pfaller proposes that interpassive art would instead "already be more than finished."[23] In the same way, God's saving work through Christ is already more than enough and will be accomplished by God, not ourselves. Even prayer, which we often think of as an interaction with God, includes a biblical element of interpassivity. Romans 8:26 describes the Holy Spirit helping our prayers when we do not know how to pray and interceding for us.

The sufficiency of God's saving action and the interpassive dynamic of delegated belief is also significant to biblical interpretation. Recent decades have seen an ongoing debate in biblical scholarship about the significance of the Pauline phrase *pistis Christou*. While sometimes translated "faith in Christ," some argue that it may be better understood as "faith/faithfulness *of* Christ," reflecting Jesus' fulfillment of God's covenant promises. In this reading, Christ believes and is faithful on our behalf, taking a priestly role as we delegate faith to our Savior. This perspective is presented in N. T. Wright's important work *Paul and the Faithfulness of God*. As Wright puts it, "Through the Messiah the prophecies have come true, the covenant has been reestablished, exile is over, God himself has acted to unveil his faithfulness to his promises, and God's people are now able . . . to keep Torah from the heart."[24]

Wright's perspective does not discount the value of human faith in God; however, it highlights the primacy of God's faithfulness to God's covenant promises and divine character. Similar to relieving the monstrous duty of appropriate response through interpassive means, delegating belief to Christ may actually enable a greater degree of trust in God's sufficiency as opposed to anxiety about the sufficiency of our own faith. As Philippians 1:6 says, "I am confident of this, that the one who began a good work in you will continue to complete it until the day of Jesus Christ." The concept of interpassivity is not merely a philosophical category that applies to digitally mediated

---

[23] Pfaller, *Interpassivity*, chapter 3.
[24] N. T. Wright, *Paul and the Faithfulness of God* (Minneapolis: Fortress, 2013), 1172.

interactions or religious rituals generally. It also provides a lens for Christian theological reflection.

Liturgical interpassivity. I want to highlight here that interpassivity is already present in our worship liturgies, regardless of digital mediation. We delegate worship to others to do it for us. While we often emphasize participation in worship, worship can be experienced simultaneously (or alternately) as production and consumption. Worship services nearly always involve both a delegation of some kind of activity or production and some kind of enjoyment, reception, or affect. We delegate the responsibility of producing worship acts such as preaching, prayer, and singing to ministers, lay leaders, and choirs; we also delegate the responsibility of experiencing worship as a receptive or consumptive experience of God's presence. Those people on the platform or stage serving as delegates and leaders (whether pastors, worship leaders, musicians, or choir members) are commonly expected not only to facilitate the participation of others but to experience something of God themselves. This experience acts as a model and provides a sense of satisfaction to observers, a sense of having offered something to God and received something from God (analogous to production and consumption; I do not mean to reduce relationship with God to capitalistic or transactional categories but to highlight the parallels with interpassivity). Singers, preachers, intercessors who offer spoken prayers, and other leaders in worship perform acts of worship both on their own behalf and especially on the behalf of the gathered worshipers. Gathered worshipers share in the communal and delegated tasks both of offering worship to God (active) and of beholding God (passive). Interpassivity is not only a postmodern phenomenon—this category can also have explanatory power around historical liturgical practices, such as placing priests in the role of receiving the Eucharist, singing or chanting liturgical texts, offering pastoral prayers, and so on.

Another example of interpassivity in worship might be engaging in a multilingual service. Even if an individual does not have the fluency to fully understand and participate in singing a song in another language, they might be encouraged and edified by experiencing the worship practices of others. Appreciating someone else worshiping in their mother tongue is interpassive, as one worshiper delegates the enjoyment of linguistic and spiritual fluency and familiarity to another, both dignifying diversity in worship and honoring God's diverse creation. Sandra Maria Van Opstal describes the significance of multicultural worship in her book *The Next Worship: Glorifying God in a Diverse World*: "Multicultural worship is not entertainment. It is an act of solidarity with communities we may never meet. It is connecting our story to their story, through which the Holy Spirit brings communion."[25] Solidarity and communion are experienced through the choice to engage in practices that are meaningful to others, even if participants accustomed to more familiar or dominant worship expressions experience discomfort. One expression of spiritual growth in such a practice can be an increase of respect for, appreciation of, and joy in others' spirituality that is expressed in unfamiliar ways.

It is also important to note that interactivity and interpassivity in worship liturgies are not reducible to a binary, good-versus-bad dynamic. Instead, both exist and interact to varying degrees in particular practices and even in the experiences of different individual worshipers engaging in the same practice. Patterns of interactivity and interpassivity in church music have changed through different approaches to liturgy and different media technologies over time. The question then becomes, How might music in the church continue to play formative, interactive and interpassive, participatory and presentational, roles in the life of communities of faith as technologies and cultures change?[26]

One such technocultural change is the advent of digital technologies and the internet. As noted previously, this change is accompanied by anxieties that online worship will be passive and therefore illegitimate. On the contrary, many passive/interpassive elements of familiar liturgical expressions occur in proximal worship. It is inaccurate to assume that in-person worship is active, and online worship is passive, per se. The proximal worship practices we are accustomed to involve both interactive and interpassive elements.

---

[25]Sandra Maria Van Opstal, *The Next Worship: Glorifying God in a Diverse World* (Downers Grove, IL: InterVarsity Press, 2015), 22.

[26]For more on categories of participatory versus presentational musicking, see Thomas Turino, *Music as Social Life: The Politics of Participation*, Chicago Studies in Ethnomusicology (Chicago: University of Chicago Press, 2008). Chapter two focuses on participatory performance, which places performers and audience on as equal ground as possible with all as essential participants, and presentational performance, which describes a dynamic in which performers and audience are clearly divided, with distinct roles.

Similarly, there is potential for meaningful interactivity and interpassivity through various media and online platforms (more on these practical opportunities later). A binary logic—one that equates active participation with only in-person worship and devalues passivity in worship as inherently lacking or even evil—is insufficient.

I also want to offer a caution and invitation to reflection for worship leaders who are often conditioned to highly prioritize active participation. Active participation in worship is often signaled by actions such as clapping, raising hands, or even jumping and dancing; at other times it is signaled by bowed posture, opened hands, closed eyes, or kneeling.[27] These various embodied and expressive responses are not evil or problematic. However, it is important to reflect on the implications of setting such a high bar for participation. There is a tendency for worship leaders to feel and impose pressure for active participation. Often this is experienced as an internal sense of guilt or anxiety. Is our worship legitimate, and is it measuring up to some standard of active participation? This can be expressed externally as projecting that guilt onto others, pressuring them to feel they should behave in certain ways.

Rather than placing a burden of participation on congregants as a way to cover up our insecurity about a lack of active engagement, I suggest that we as worship leaders can spend less time and energy on the *should* and more on the *why*. We can ask what barriers there might be to interactive participation and how we might lower them. We can also reflect on what might be appropriate interpassive modes of participation and how to encourage them in ways that provide space for people to support each other in encountering God. Perhaps there are ways in which we can move away from placing pressure on individual affective experience and toward communal practice and sharing as the criteria of worship.

THE SECOND BINARY: EMBODIED VERSUS DISEMBODIED

On January 30, 2022, author and priest (of the Anglican Church in North America) Tish Harrison Warren published an opinion piece in the *New York*

---

[27]Miranda Klaver, "Worship Music as Aesthetic Domain of Meaning and Bonding: The Glocal Context of a Dutch Pentecostal Church," in *The Spirit of Praise: Music and Worship in Global Pentecostal-Charismatic Christianity*, ed. Monique Marie Ingalls and Amos Yong (University Park: Pennsylvania State University Press, 2015), 104-5.

Times with the headline "Why Churches Should Drop Their Online Services." Warren wrote as someone who supported churches going online during the early stages of the pandemic in response to the health risks associated with in-person gatherings. Warren stated:

> I think it's time to drop the virtual option. And I think this for the same reason I believed churches should go online back in March 2020: This is the way to love God and our neighbors.
>
> For all of us—even those who aren't churchgoers—bodies, with all the risk, danger, limits, mortality and vulnerability that they bring, are part of our deepest humanity, not obstacles to be transcended through digitization. They are humble (and humbling) gifts to be embraced. Online church, while it was necessary for a season, diminishes worship and us as people. We seek to worship wholly—with heart, soul, mind and strength—and embodiment is an irreducible part of that wholeness.[28]

Returning to in-person-only worship was, for Warren, a matter of loving God and neighbor, because of the importance of embodiment. In Warren's view, embodiment is diminished through digitization, which represents an attempt to "transcend" physicality. Warren highlights the importance of physical human connection, felt keenly during the pandemic. She names the cost of being apart, and the need for tangible human interaction and presence.

While Warren's statements about the importance of human connection are true, many scholars would dispute her conclusions regarding the relationship between embodiment and digital media. These conclusions led her to reject an ongoing online presence for churches, saying that continuing to offer an online option "makes embodiment elective," a "consumer preference."[29] For Warren, embodiment is an option chosen by those who attend church in person and rejected by those who view a service online. In a certain sense, Warren is correct: if someone does not attend a church service in person, they are not interacting with their fellow congregants in the physical ways we do when we share the same space. This is a real difference, and it is significant.

Warren ends her article with this statement: "A chief thing that the church has to offer the world now is to remind us all how to be human creatures, with

---

[28]Tish Harrison Warren, "Why Churches Should Drop Their Online Services," *New York Times*, January 30, 2022, www.nytimes.com/2022/01/30/opinion/church-online-services-covid.html.
[29]Warren, "Why Churches Should Drop Their Online Services."

all the embodiment and physical limits that implies. We need to embrace that countercultural call."[30] Again, her implication seems to be that reminders of our humanity, and embodiment more broadly, happen in person and do not happen (or are diminished) online. Warren assumes that *digital* is synonymous with *disembodied*, and *in person* with *embodied*.

A myriad of Christian theologians would agree that bodies and embodiment *are* hugely important, even essential, to Christian faith, discipleship, and worship.[31] We also *should* seek to worship with all that we are, and embodiment is a necessary part of holistic worship. Where Warren departs from the findings of much recent scholarship is in her suggestion that removing online engagement is the path to wholeness. In what follows, I will argue that instead of being a diminishment and obstacle to embodiment, digital engagement is inherently embodied and is a part of our holistic discipleship. Removing digital realities from our faith is in fact an amputation of an important part of our cultural experience from our life together with each other and with God. The choice between online and offline ministry is (ironically) not a binary one.

The question raised by digital technologies is how these new media forms interface with our experience of embodiment. Popular Christian discourse around embodiment since the Covid-19 pandemic is lacking in several ways. Many Christians may not actually quite know what they mean by *embodiment* when they use the term. Embodiment has the potential to become a category that lacks clarity and precision and can thereby be used to shore up whatever practices or habits of thought we find comfortable and familiar, without examining their drawbacks and shortcomings. Additionally, conversations within church settings about embodiment as it relates to worship often display little if any engagement

---

[30] Warren, "Why Churches Should Drop Their Online Services."
[31] Sources on this topic include: Teresa Berger, @ *Worship: Liturgical Practices in Digital Worlds*, Liturgy, Worship, and Society (New York: Routledge, 2018); James W. Jones, *Living Religion: Embodiment, Theology, and the Possibility of a Spiritual Sense* (New York: Oxford University Press, 2019); Peter Phillips, "Digital Being," *Crucible*, January 2023, https://crucible.hymnsam.co.uk/articles/2023/january/articles/digital-being/; Ola Sigurdson, "How to Speak of the Body? Embodiment Between Phenomenology and Theology," *Studia Theologica* 62, no. 1 (2008): 25-43; Marcell Silva Steuernagel, *Church Music Through the Lens of Performance*, Congregational Music Studies (London; Routledge, 2021); Hannah Lyn Venable, "The Weight of Bodily Presence in Art and Liturgy," *Religions* 12, no. 3 (2021): 164.

Activity and Embodiment

with various disciplines of study, whether centered on music performance, neuroscience, or sustained theological reflection.[32] Many of us have had meaningful experiences of shared song in corporate worship; these moments can become powerful touchstones of what it means to be engaged in the worship of God with our whole selves, and rightly so. However, there is more to the interaction of human bodies, music, and technology than we often consider.

In what follows, I will explore several topics related to embodiment that are worthy of our attention as we consider what the future of the church's musical worship may look like. First, I will explore perspectives from musicologists about the ways humans embody music. The human body is involved in all kinds of music making, listening, learning, and imagining. This will lead into my second point, which relates to how technologies are implicated in embodiment. Third, I will offer a challenge to the church to take the opportunity afforded by the change brought about during the pandemic to approach its understanding and practice of embodiment in more inclusive and accessible ways. Fourth, I will discuss developing theological perspectives on embodiment in a digital age. Our imaginations of what it means to be embodied humans will need to grow and change as the world we live in changes.

EMBODIMENT AND MUSIC MAKING

Ramón Pelinski writes, "Until the last decades of the 20th Century talking about embodiment was an impertinence in musicology. . . . 'Musicking' or listening to music were seen as disembodied activities obviously controlled by such superior instances as spirit, soul, or (if possible) pure reason."[33] These words highlight a dynamic present in some (though not all) discussions and perceptions of music. Even on a popular level, we may talk about a musical performance as a "transcendent" or "out-of-body" experience. Particularly within the Western classical tradition, there have been ideological and methodological pressures to treat music as an object of intellectualized study, fixated more on written musical scores than on the

---

[32]See Steuernagel, *Church Music Through the Lens of Performance*.
[33]Ramón Pelinski, "Embodiment and Musical Experience," *Trans* 9 (2005), www.sibetrans.com/trans/articulo/178/embodiment-and-musical-experience.

bodies and communities where that music came to life and affected human lives.

Pelinski writes about ways that embodiment affects musical experience, including "as an innate bodily schema." The body schema is a kind of blueprint of possibilities for a human body within a cultural environment. Pelinski imagines a young musician entering into their first cello lessons. The body schema, in this case, includes the student making movements appropriate to their cultural context and the task at hand: sitting in a chair, holding their instrument with proper technique, and so on.[34] A body schema allows a person to respond preconceptually to the cultural possibilities inherent in an object, such as a musical instrument. An instrument is a physical piece of technology that provides possibilities for the music student to expand their musical capacities and experiences.

The body schema facilitates the development of physical abilities through practice, leading to habitual learning and muscle memory.[35] In an important sense, music education is physical education. Learning to sing or to play an instrument is not a matter of comprehending principles of technique, music theory, or melodic and harmonic material. Instead, it is a set of muscular movements that are finely honed through training to produce extremely specific and yet flexible physical outcomes that can be applied in a wide variety of scenarios. Learning music is only possible through embodiment; in fact, this process of learning changes our experience of embodiment. Pelinski claims, "Musical performance habits transform and enrich the body schema. Thanks to them, the musical instrument integrates itself into the performer's body as an extension of it."[36]

This experience of extended or expanded embodiment through the acquisition of musical habits is at least partly why I say "ouch" and feel an instinctive sense of shock or pain if I bump my violin or guitar and risk damaging it. My body feels protective of these technologies external to me because they are no longer perceived as something external. After decades of musical training and practice, the violin and guitar are parts of my body schema, my sense of self, and my experience of embodiment. I have lived as

---

[34] Pelinski, "Embodiment and Musical Experience."
[35] Pelinski, "Embodiment and Musical Experience."
[36] Pelinski, "Embodiment and Musical Experience."

an embodied person who plays musical instruments far longer than I have lived as an embodied person who does not. To harm my instrument is to harm me by limiting the potential expression of my embodiment.

Eugene Montague argues that the entrainment of repeated physical actions in making music leads to the development of "a specific bodily ability, much like athletic training in a gym.... Musical disciplines develop particular movements that come to define bodies."[37] These bodily abilities are developed first as discrete physical actions, each learned and practiced carefully and with intention. However, as they become integrated into the body schema, these movements become subconscious. Subconscious integration is necessary to attaining mastery of an instrument; it would be impractical to play complex music while remaining consciously aware of every specific aspect of technique. The performer no longer understands a piece of music as a sequence of bodily movements but "as a flow of sounds" that they instinctually embody.[38] Learning to play an instrument is not less embodied because it involves technology; rather, the process of attaining greater mastery over that technology represents an increased experience of embodiment.

This discussion of integrating skills, movements, and ways of being into our subconscious functioning and experience may sound familiar. It is the same process new technologies go through as they become invisible and come to be perceived as a natural or given part of our world, discussed in chapter one.[39] When a technology, whether a saxophone or a smartphone, becomes part of our body schema, it falls out of our conscious attention and allows us to experience embodiment in new ways. Additionally, the potential body schema related to a given technology is not fixed; for instance, instrumentalists such as violinist Nicolò Paganini and pianist Franz Liszt pushed the boundaries of what was possible with their technology of choice, opening new potentialities for musicians who came after them. This raises the question how we might gain greater fluency and capacity with various technologies, while also exploring new possibilities for those technologies in order to better use them for the purpose of ministry.

---

[37] Eugene Montague, "Entrainment and Embodiment in Musical Performance," in *The Oxford Handbook of Music and the Body*, ed. Youn Kim and Sander L. Gilman (Oxford: Oxford University Press, 2019), 183.
[38] Montague, "Entrainment and Embodiment," 184.
[39] Gray Young, ed., *The Internet*, The Reference Shelf 70 (New York: H. W. Wilson, 1998), vii.

EMBODIMENT AND MUSIC LISTENING

While we may be in general agreement that making music is undoubtedly embodied, experiences of listening to music may seem less clearly so. Listening to music may strike us as, at least in some cases, passive, disconnected, and even disembodied. Musicologist and pianist Hamish J. Robb argues, however, that this is not the case. Even when we listen to music, we understand the sounds we hear partly through our mirroring of the embodied experience of the person creating that music. Robb points out, "Studies show that motor areas of the brain activate when merely imagining movements such as those used in music performance."[40] On this account, we embody music in order to hear it, not only to create it. In fact, hearing music is itself, perhaps to varying degrees, an act of co-creation. Cognitive scientist Gregory A. Bryant writes, "Bodies generate rhythms through specialized motor programs, often with the help of culturally evolved technology, and drive perceptually guided action. Even passive listening to musical rhythms will activate motor areas of the brain."[41] Bryant's language of "specialized motor programs" helped by "culturally evolved technology" apparently describes something nearly equivalent to a body schema. Even listening to music requires a trained set of bodily responses that help us make sense of sound *as* music.

As we make meaning of music through our embodied response to sound, we empathically simulate the embodiment of the performers. Robb suggest this simulation can occur both through actually seeing performers and through imagining their physical motions if they are not in view (as we might while listening to a recording). According to Robb, this is part of what gives music its power to *move* us, both in terms of physical motion and emotional resonance. Indeed, motion and emotion are deeply intertwined, as the activity of mirror neurons helps our brains to understand both the physical movements and the feelings of others.[42]

Robb goes on to describe how a listener might simulate and embody the physical actions of a horn player executing a rising melodic gesture. As the

---
[40] Hamish Robb, "Imagined, Supplemental Sound in Nineteenth-Century Piano Music: Towards a Fuller Understanding of Musical Embodiment," *Music Theory Online* 21, no. 3 (2015), https://mtosmt.org/issues/mto.15.21.3/mto.15.21.3.robb.html.
[41] Gregory Bryant, "Rhythm and the Body," in *A Multidisciplinary Approach to Embodiment: Understanding Human Being*, ed. Nancy Kimberly Dess (New York: Routledge, 2021), 66-67.
[42] Robb, "Imagined, Supplemental Sound."

horn player exerts greater effort in producing the required air pressure to support the sound, the listener experiences a version of this exertion within their own body. The same can occur with instruments such as the piano, which do not require differentiated levels of energy for high and low pitches per se. In this case, the pianist may create the illusion of effort as a mode of increasing musical expressiveness, and the listener will respond in kind.[43] The tension and release inherent within music is felt, and even produced, within our own listening bodies. As we listen to another person sing, the muscles of our vocal mechanism and diaphragm contract to mirror the performer's embodiment, even if we make no sound (this is called subvocalization). The same phenomenon also commonly occurs with instrumental music.

It is worth nothing that the degree of felt co-agency in music listeners is not always the same; rather, it depends on the degree and intensity of the individual's engagement with the music. Sociologist of the arts Mia Nakamura states, "Embodied response differs according to one's degree of involvement with sound. . . . Rhythmic entrainment and recalling an episodic memory are also induced in casual listening, but whole-body coordination and deep reflection are brought about only by focused listening." Nakamura concludes that, while every level of musical engagement does entail embodied response, that response differs. She offers categories of "unconscious response, passive listening, active listening, participation, and absorbed participation" as points along a spectrum of involvement.[44]

This raises interesting questions for worship leaders. If even listening to music passively generates physical responses in our bodies, how might this inform our understanding of participation in gathered worship? When we look out at a congregation of believers and see some who are singing with gusto, while others are apparently less engaged, what invitation might there be to bring curiosity to our response? Can we lay down the monstrous burden of anxiety that tells us their lack of obvious, outward embodied response is a sign of failure or even a threat? Might we have a conversation with that person that does not start with the assumption that they dislike us or

---

[43] Robb, "Imagined, Supplemental Sound."
[44] Mia Nakamura, "Music Sociology Meets Neuroscience," in Kim and Gilman, *Oxford Handbook*, 132-33.

disapprove of our ministry, and instead ask questions such as, "What are you thinking or praying about when we worship together?" or "What do you feel in your body and heart when we are gathered?"

EMBODYING INCLUSION

Various forms of technology and media are ubiquitous in our worship practices. Some of these are new, exciting, or uncomfortable. Others are so normalized to us that they become invisible. However, invisible technologies do not only allow for possibilities of human connection and expression; they also pose risks of exclusion. If we become so accustomed to the technologies, structures, and systems we use that we no longer perceive them fully, this may also lead to our failing to see where those structures fall short. The questions raised by digital church offer an opportunity for us to reexamine our practices of worship and what expressions of embodiment they privilege and marginalize. When we say, "embodiment matters, therefore we have to go back to meeting as we did before," one of the implications is that we value bodies that those environments are designed for more than bodies that have historically been excluded by the physical contours of our practices. For the church to truly value embodiment as important to its music and worship, it must be willing to ask *how* embodiment matters and *whose* bodies matter.

Amy Kenny writes honestly and incisively on the ways Christian institutions have excluded and harmed disabled people in her book *My Body Is Not a Prayer Request: Disability Justice in the Church*. Among other topics, Kenny describes the unfortunate history of the church opposing civil rights for disabled people. She writes that many churches "have absorbed the core spiritual lie known as ableism," evidenced by some churches' opposition to the Americans with Disabilities Act (ADA). The ADA excluded religious communities from its purview, influenced by that opposition from Christian leaders. These leaders condemned the ADA as "imposing burdensome costs . . . [and] needless injury to religious exercise." Kenny summarizes poignantly: "The message was clear: we are simply not worth the cost. Money was more important than disabled people."[45]

---

[45] Amy Kenny, *My Body Is Not a Prayer Request: Disability Justice in the Church* (Grand Rapids, MI: Baker Books, 2022), 27-28.

The church should be wary of how it leverages the importance of embodiment in worship, lest it fall into the error of using embodiment as an excuse to devalue and exclude human bodies, as it used religious liberty in opposing the ADA. Kenny's testimony is an important warning to the church. She notes, "Evidently, our very presence diminished the ability of others to worship. . . . The erasure of disability in church spaces was deliberately manufactured because disabled people were (and still are) considered too pricey and profane to include." Kenny expresses the hurt that religious liberty was used in such an exclusionary way and names the discouraging reality of this ongoing legal norm.[46]

The church has work to do repenting of ableism, healing the harm it has caused, and advocating for the rights and loving inclusion of all people. At the same time, there are also opportunities for the church to find new ways to care for people who have been excluded. Do we consider people with different physical and sensory needs when we decide what our musical worship will look and sound like? Is our interest in accommodating disabled people in our churches limited to having a space for them in the congregation (if we even do that), or do we build our sanctuaries, chapels, and worship centers with the expectation that disabled people will *lead* in worship? Are we willing to prioritize this in our planning, building, and use of funds, as well as in creative problem solving when those pursuits have fallen short of inclusion?

While digital expressions of church may sometimes be perceived as a threat to embodiment, they may in fact provide one way forward (among multiple) for embodying inclusion and including all bodies. Virtual reality pastor DJ Soto has experienced these possibilities. When I interviewed Soto, he described how ministering to homebound individuals has become a life-giving and positive aspect of virtual reality church. Numerous believers are unable to physically attend church for a myriad of reasons. Soto names the expectation that people have to come *to* the church, with the possible accommodation of a minister visiting the homebound as an exception to "normal" ministry. Virtual reality church flips the familiar script, allowing people to participate on equal footing regardless of experiences that would limit them

---

[46]Kenny, *My Body Is Not a Prayer Request*, 29.

from physically showing up to and navigating a building on a Sunday morning. Soto celebrates the meaningful experience of engaging with people through virtual reality in immersive, face-to-face interactions.[47]

Of course, virtual reality is not the only solution. However, it is instructive to consider the implications of embodiment in digital space. The previous discussion of music and embodiment highlights that developing body schemas that integrate facility with new technology, imagined or virtual movement and sound, and even listening are all embodied processes. If our concepts of embodiment have no room for digital technology, perhaps it is not that unfamiliar technocultural expressions are illegitimate, but that our frameworks require expansion. Soto highlights the knee-jerk response he often encounters in discussing his work:

> I'm noticing the church—and I'm speaking very broadly—has an automated negative reaction towards the digital embodiment of an individual. And so there's an automatic negative reaction to it without even experiencing it. And so [they say] things like, you know, "They're not connected. How can you have discipleship? How can you have relationships?"[48]

Soto argues, however, that relational Christian practices such as discipleship and worship can occur through digital media, and that our habitual choices of technology in proximal worship practices may not be as successful as we like to assume. He challenges churches to "take an honest look at [the] current physical church" and be willing to reevaluate just how welcoming, engaging, and interactive our practices are for a new person walking through the doors. Soto points out that it is completely possible and even common to experience church in physical proximity in ways that are shallow and perfunctory: "When you look at the interaction level of a physical event on Sunday morning, it's not like we're blowing it out of the water."[49]

In Soto's experience of virtual reality church, those baseline social interactions of greetings and conversations can still happen. Similar to a three-dimensional video game, people can walk into a VR space with their avatar much as they would in a church building, and can speak to and be heard by others. However, the virtual reality relationships "have the tendency to go

---

[47]DJ Soto, interview by author, Zoom, January 13, 2023.
[48]Soto, interview.
[49]Soto, interview.

Activity and Embodiment

way beyond" surface-level introductions. Soto cites several reasons, noting the degree of safety for some participants brought by having an avatar in virtual reality. People visiting a church on Sunday often enter with the expectation that they will be judged based on their appearance and that personal interactions will be only skin deep. However, Soto has found that, time after time, people in the virtual reality spaces where he ministers will say, "I wouldn't be able to talk about this in the physical church," because of cultural and personal barriers, but will feel comfortable sharing with much greater vulnerability and authenticity. He acknowledges that this dynamic does come down to the culture of a given space and community, and that people can certainly have negative experiences of community in metaverse spaces. But Soto concludes, "At a fundamental baseline level, you're going to have a higher level of interaction because of the nature of the technology, because of the anonymity of the avatar."[50]

Soto is careful to highlight that he does not pit virtual reality church/metaverse church against physical church meetings in steepled buildings. Rather, he suggests that both serve valuable purposes, and each is suited to its own context and can reach particular people and situations well. Soto says that metaverse spaces are not necessarily better than physical spaces of worship, but each serves exceptionally well in different scenarios. For instance, Soto says, "For people who are homebound, this metaverse thing is the answer. It is the solution for them." Soto hopes that believers will not disqualify this kind of experience as illegitimate discipleship or unsuited to spiritual growth. He describes how people who have been excluded from the church can experience community and connection in new ways: "They can come in, let's say their body is . . . confined in a wheelchair. They can run all around, walk around, hang out, volunteer, preach, teach, be a greeter. The world is just opened up for them to that degree."[51]

The broader church still has much to consider and make sense of regarding the value and significance of digital embodiment, but I suggest that there remains much conversation to be had about its potential. At the same time, we should not use the existence of virtual reality as an excuse to abdicate responsibility for inclusivity and accessibility in our physical. My goal

---

[50]Soto, interview.
[51]Soto, interview.

is not to say that the future of the church is only online or only in virtual reality or the metaverse. However, if we claim to value embodiment, the example of Christ calls us to make the last to be first in this way: we should *begin* our conversations about embodiment with the experiences of those whose bodies have been excluded and make sure we are doing all we can to include them. If we do this, we will truly be valuing embodiment in our worship.

In her research with the Exploring the Pandemic Impact on Congregations project, Allison Norton has seen this negotiation happen in churches of a variety of sizes, from megachurches to small, rural congregations. Some of these small congregations, which Norton points out are more typical congregations in the United States, are predominantly sixty-five or older, and many members are homebound. Norton describes several congregations that decided "we're a better online church than face to face." These churches could sell their building, meet predominantly through a platform such as Zoom, and avoid travel that might be dangerous or unmanageable for many of their members. Norton enthusiastically reports that these congregations are thriving and realizing that this new model of gathering is a better fit for their community. Contrary to what many of us might expect or think of when we hear the phrase "online church," these are not megachurches but churches of fifty or fewer members, mostly seniors, who experienced tangible benefits such as not needing to travel in the winter and being able to include people who could never participate in a traditional church gathering. These people often fall through the cracks of our familiar models of church but have found meaningful ways to build community online.[52]

Norton notes that this renegotiation "includes people with special needs in certain cases as well." One member of a study told Norton how their ADHD made sitting through a Sunday service an unpleasant and unmanageable endeavor. This congregant was able to participate equally with others in a Zoom church setting, which enabled her to be active out in nature while simultaneously connected with her church community in worship.[53] Whether people experience geographic distance, job-related restrictions on church attendance, or mental or physical obstacles to participating in

---
[52] Allison Norton, interview by author, Zoom, February 23, 2023.
[53] Norton, interview.

Activity and Embodiment

expected embodied ways, there may yet be room for the church to expand its embrace of Christ's body.

THEOLOGY OF DIGITAL EMBODIMENT

If we aspire to this kind of embrace, what might the implications be for our theology? Peter Phillips works as the program director for the master of arts in digital theology at Spurgeon's College in London. He is an advocate of hybrid ministry expressions and is committed to theological reflection on the implications of digital media and technology for the church's worship and witness. As he teaches ministers regarding the use of digital technologies in the church, he has ample opportunity to articulate the theological significance of those technologies and their use. In January 2023, Phillips wrote an article for *Crucible* magazine titled "Digital Being." Phillips acknowledges the critiques leveled at digital expressions of church, based on assumptions that they are not "real church" or that because of the nature of embodiment they are "second best." Phillips questions "whether public critique of online church has fully engaged with digital being and our experience of 'being human in a digital age.'"[54]

Many of these critiques center on the charge that participants in digitally mediated religious practices are not engaging in the embodied reality of church. Phillips sees these practices differently. He writes, "In both online and onsite church activities participants are always embodied, always in person: digital being is just another mode of embodiment." Phillips claims that "transcending" embodiment is something we regularly do; we are imaginative and creative as well as embodied, and we participate in the divine attributes of transcendence and immanence. Phillips offers a clear rebuttal to popular suspicions about digital disembodiment:

> It is our bodies which always operate technology through our physical attributes whether that technology is the hymnbook or the keyboard.... To say that those worshipping online divest their physical identity for something more gnostic, more digital, less embodied, is a fundamental misunderstanding of how we exist/act/worship as human beings. To be online is to be as embodied, as open to God, as human, as vulnerable, as real, as it is to be onsite.[55]

---

[54]Phillips, "Digital Being," 22.
[55]Phillips, "Digital Being," 25.

Online interactions, Phillips argues, are an essential part of our radically contextual experience. Just as we cannot ignore the social, cultural, and theological context of our churches as we minister, we likewise are bound to our technological context, which is implicated in every layer of our situatedness. Phillips contends that all of our relationships are "part of the mediated construction of our own contextual reality which is part and parcel of our embodiment *in media res* amidst the techno-natural world. . . . Digital being is an embodied experience as much as any other expression . . . [in] our context."[56]

Phillips reinforces the importance of embodiment in both online and offline human experiences and interactions. In his view, human beings "can never not be real," whether mediated or not. We cannot survive and exist except as embodied beings. Phillips spoke with me about what this framing means for the church's worship, saying, "Human beings are always . . . flesh and embodied, even when they're appearing on Zoom." For Phillips, this essential embodiment of humans at all times will affect how the church navigates worship, how we value these kinds of interactions, and even thorny issues such as sacraments.[57] The specifics of how these embodied online experiences will play out and will be narrated theologically will vary based on the given context of each worshiping community and tradition. But we must acknowledge at the start that digital being and media interpenetrate most, if not all, of those worship contexts to some degree.

This overlapping of the digital into our other experiences is not new since the Covid-19 pandemic. In her 2018 book @ *Worship: Liturgical Practices in Digital Worlds*, Catholic theologian and scholar Teresa Berger already was reflecting and writing on these issues. Experiences of digital religion were not yet as prolific and normalized as they have become, but they were active and growing. Berger tackles one common objection to these experiences: "When critics of digitally mediated liturgical practices insist that such worship happens 'without the requirement of a physically present body,' this claim is far too un-nuanced. There always has to be a 'physically present' body to enter into worship online."[58] According to Berger, "both online and

---

[56]Phillips, "Digital Being," 29.
[57]Peter Phillips, interview by author, Zoom, March 1, 2023.
[58]Berger, @ *Worship*, 19.

Activity and Embodiment

offline praying involves human bodies and a range of other materialities." Given how closely interwoven our physical and digital lives are today, it becomes difficult and even unproductive to draw a clear boundary between what is embodied and what is not based on digital mediation. As Berger puts it, "Rather than being fundamentally disembodied, digitally mediated worship entails its own specific bodily proprieties. These are governed on the one hand by what new media technologies facilitate and on the other hand by the bodily particulars of worshippers who enter digitally mediated sacred spaces."[59]

Part of the challenge of navigating questions of participation and embodiment in the twenty-first century, in the midst of a technological revolution, is that the church's existing categories for understanding participation and embodiment have not previously needed to account for the new variables introduced by digital technology. Berger references the twentieth-century liturgical renewal's emphasis on "*actuosa participatio*," closely related to the concern for "full, conscious, active participation" noted above in Vatican II. Berger writes that this ideal participant was generated by modern norms that "privileged images of a self that is stable, bounded, self-determining, unencumbered, and also—though this remains largely hidden—able-bodied, neurotypical, and dominantly male."[60]

Berger's insight highlights the forms of embodiment the church has historically valued and centered. The challenges facing the church in the early 2020s, while daunting, may also provide opportunities for repentance, restructuring of power and access, and creating more just and loving forms of worship. The church is invited to greater attentiveness and deeper reflection on the incarnational ministry to which it is called. Rather than a top-down, prescriptive model for embodied participation that imposes heavy burdens on others without making necessary sacrifices to help them (Matthew 23:4), the church must embrace an inclusive, empowering vision that lifts up those entrusted to its care and invites them to come to God as they are. The church's worship can and should be offered to God in ways that welcome and nurture the affective and physical wholeness and discipleship of believers.

---

[59] Berger, *@ Worship*, 20-21.
[60] Berger, *@ Worship*, 22.

I have argued in this chapter that the church's approach to worship has at times strayed into placing burdens on the hearts of its people and constructing barriers to their embodied belonging. The tumultuous change of the 2020s has stripped bare some of these harmful practices. Perhaps in the wake of the storm, the church can reflect on how it can better serve God's children and rebuild a house of worship more aligned with God's loving reign.

Mediation and Virtuality

MEDIA AND MEDIATION ARE INTRIGUINGLY flexible terms. We speak of media as tools used to accomplish tasks, as forms of artistic expression, and as industries that communicate news to mass audiences. Mediation implies being between things or people, but this can be seen as negative or positive. Mediation can refer to a barrier preventing face-to-face connection, or to a helpful go-between for two parties who could not see eye to eye on their own. Even in religious settings, mediation is an important and sometimes contested category. Some religious traditions emphasize the role of mediators between human beings and the divine, while others minimize them. What are we to make of media and mediation when it comes to worship?

THE THIRD BINARY: MEDIATED VERSUS UNMEDIATED

There are many potential versions of what the ideal worshiper or worship experience looks like. All of them might well be critiqued and problematized, and simultaneously many have positive gifts to offer to the church in its worship and witness. If you search Google for images related to "worship," you will likely find an array of photos of a crowd of people silhouetted by bright stage lights at what appears to be a megachurch or concert venue. Other search results might include occasional exceptions depicting an individual, perhaps kneeling, in an outdoor, natural setting with hands raised. This cultural depiction is dominated by evangelical faith expressions, most significantly through music in settings involving significant high-production-value multimedia. The imagined worshiper who sings to God with outstretched arms, closed eyes, and impassioned emotions may be focused upward (or inward); however, this ideal is commonly associated with a particular media environment.[1]

Given how important these aesthetic musical elements are to the construction of faith-based narratives and identities of evangelical worshipers, one might expect a large amount of focus to be placed on music and music leaders within evangelical discourse. In part this does occur, but it exists in a curious tension with a contrasting desire to minimize the role of music and musicians in worship. Monique Ingalls describes the evangelical worship experience as "an affective time of personal communion with God mediated through contemporary worship music," and while this description certainly is accurate, it stands in paradox with other elements of evangelical experience and lexicon.[2] Joshua Busman describes the goal of evangelical worship as achieving "'true worship,' usually defined as an unmediated encounter with God."[3] Marcell Steuernagel recounts statements from evangelical leaders reflecting music as "immediate . . . palpable, and concrete," in contrast to language.[4] Miranda Klaver points out, "Worshippers recall the encounter with the sacred as an immediate and unmediated experience. However, processes of mediation are always at play in the domain of religion . . . because the sacred requires some media forms in order to be experienced and understood by believers."[5] Music, then, functions in evangelical worship as mediated access to an aspirationally unmediated experience of the divine.

Busman engages further with this perplexing contradiction through the concept of "vanishing mediators." He contends, "Worship bands and the

---

[1] Monique Ingalls has offered a similar analysis of Google images with a slightly different emphasis in *Singing the Congregation: How Contemporary Worship Music Forms Evangelical Community* (New York: Oxford University Press, 2018), 17.
[2] Monique Marie Ingalls, "Worship on Screen: Building Networked Congregations Through Audiovisual Worship Media," in *Singing the Congregation*, 174.
[3] Joshua Kalin Busman, "(Re)Sounding Passion: Listening to American Evangelical Worship Music, 1997–2015" (PhD diss., University of North Carolina at Chapel Hill, 2015), 146.
[4] Marcell Silva Steuernagel, *Church Music Through the Lens of Performance*, Congregational Music Studies (London; Routledge, 2021), 91, 94.
[5] Miranda Klaver, "Worship Music as Aesthetic Domain of Meaning and Bonding: The Glocal Context of a Dutch Pentecostal Church," in *The Spirit of Praise: Music and Worship in Global Pentecostal-Charismatic Christianity*, ed. Monique Marie Ingalls and Amos Yong (University Park: Pennsylvania State University Press, 2015), 109.

Mediation and Virtuality

songs they sing serve as 'vanishing mediators' between their congregations to the divine." A vanishing mediator is "a person, idea, or institution that transforms one social order into another and immediately disappears once the transformation is completed. In fact, the transformation of one sociality into another is often predicated upon the disappearance of the mediator." Busman argues that praise and worship music and worship leaders are vanishing mediators—necessary to the experience of worship but successful only insofar as they accomplish their own erasure, "leaving only a fully transparent connection point between fan-worshippers and the divine."[6] Thus, mediated music in evangelical worship functions to build a multilayered framework of sensory, emotional, and conceptual experiences that reinforce each other. The industry of worship music and the professional worship leaders who front the industry's products seek to craft musical experiences that achieve either the perception or the reality of unmediated encounter with God, through the use of media.

This dynamic of vanishing mediators maps closely onto the concept, discussed previously, of technologies becoming invisible. A worshiper in a mediated worship environment must first develop fluency in the mediated, cultural expressions within a particular set of semiotic markers used in worship (music, style, language, architecture, etc.). Engaging with these *technologies* to the fullest extent requires a degree of familiarity and even skill. Only then can the "music fade," along with the rest of the deeply mediated experience of sharing human culture, allowing the illusion of unmediated encounter to materialize.[7]

In pursuit of the goal of unmediated encounter with the divine, both the media and the mediators of that experience are made invisible, even if they are still present and active. Klaver describes this paradox in a different way, highlighting "the reception of the program [of evangelical worship] as immediate and unmediated, divine experiences by the audiences," in contrast with the meticulous planning required and the "mediation through music and new media wrapped in idioms closely related to popular culture." More directly related to concerns for leaders, the

---

[6] Busman, "(Re)Sounding Passion," 163-64.
[7] Busman, "(Re)Sounding Passion," 164. Busman references Matt Redman's song "The Heart of Worship," which begins with the lyrics "When the music fades / All is stripped away."

audience/congregation is expected to engage their inner selves emotionally and express this unmediated experience externally; worship pastors and musicians are often pressured to tightly control their own experiences and expressiveness, lest they throw a wrench in the finely tuned invisible machine of mediated worship.[8]

This raises the question of what we mean by *media* in the word's common usage. Most likely, when used in popular conversation and even conversations around the church's music, *media* implicitly refers to "media technologies," by which we mean relatively recent technologies, such as computers, smartphones, the internet, and digital media, that are not yet invisible to us *as* technologies. It is unlikely that many people referring to "worship media" are thinking of hymnals, stained glass, incense, and church pews, though these are all examples of media used in worship. Digital media as a broad class represent our most recent collective experience of mediation (with subsets such as social media and virtual reality being even newer expressions) and have become what we think of as media. But this is still only part of the picture.

Questions remain concerning whether "unmediated worship" is even possible or desirable, the ubiquity of mediation in music (and the rest of our lived experiences), and implications for reconsidering worship in the midst of a media revolution. Worship is always mediated and always has been. Mediation is not a bad thing but, crucially, the way we enter into relationship with God.

THE IMPOSSIBLE DREAM: UNMEDIATED WORSHIP

Teresa Berger has written extensively about the relationship between worship and media. In her book @ *Worship: Liturgical Practices in Digital Worlds*, Berger argues that mediation is an intrinsic part of human worship of the divine, not a recent introduction of something unnatural. Berger writes, "There is no original, pristine moment in liturgical history when worship stood apart from media forms. . . . Digital media technologies stand in a long line of liturgical mediations—without which there is no im/*media*/cy of

---

[8]Miranda Klaver, *This Is My Desire: A Semiotic Perspective on Conversion in an Evangelical Seeker Church and a Pentecostal Church in the Netherlands* (Amsterdam: Pallas, 2011), 155-56.

Mediation and Virtuality

encounter with the divine." Berger concludes that it is no longer useful to draw a hard line between "'natural' on the one hand and 'artificial/technological/human-made' on the other hand" because "there is no unmediated bodily presence at worship, offline or offline. . . . No worship occurs without media and mediation."[9]

Even though these categories of natural and technological are becoming less clear, many Christians still attempt to interpret the world through them. In order for church leaders and scholars to reflect productively on the significance of mediation in worship, we must first accept the presence of media in all we do. Peter Phillips's 2023 article "Digital Being" highlights the inescapability of media technology in our worship experiences, including "microphones, audio devices, headphones, hearing aids, glasses, televisions, screens (onsite and online), cameras and the theatre of the liturgy and architecture itself."[10] Our mediated, sensory experience is inextricable from our spiritual, religious experience.

This claim may sound counterintuitive to our experiences of religion, especially given the ideals of unmediated encounter with God discussed previously. However, sociocultural anthropologist Marleen de Witte suggests media are not "something new and external to religion, but . . . intrinsic to religion as a practice of mediation. . . . Religion always needs media."[11] These media, whether ProPresenter slides, a hymnbook, an altar or pulpit, a practiced ritual or gesture, or a YouTube stream, can also become sites of conflict. Which forms of mediation represent legitimate spiritual encounter, and which are perceived as barriers to connection with the divine and with community? De Witte sees modern media technologies such as radio and television as similar to older, more familiar mediations. She also points out that once media become accepted practice, the fact that they do mediate is minimized: "Religious practitioners call upon media to define, construct, and experience their relationship with the spiritual world, but sacralize or

---

[9]Teresa Berger, @ *Worship: Liturgical Practices in Digital Worlds*, Liturgy, Worship, and Society (New York: Routledge, 2018), 7, 19-20.

[10]Peter Phillips, "Digital Being," *Crucible*, January 2023, https://crucible.hymnsam.co.uk/articles/2023/january/articles/digital-being/.

[11]Marleen de Witte, "Modes of Binding, Moments of Bonding. Mediating Divine Touch in Ghanaian Pentecostalism and Traditionalism," in *Aesthetic Formations: Media, Religion, and the Senses*, ed. Birgit Meyer (New York: Palgrave Macmillan, 2009), 185.

naturalize these media so as to authenticate religious experiences as immediate and 'real.'"[12]

Here we return to the idea of a vanishing mediator or invisible technology. Musical worship is a practice deeply embedded within the mediations and technologies that give shape to our experience of the world and human relationships. The materiality of worship means mediation is unavoidable. But perhaps we do not need to try to erase worship's various mediators from our vision. In what follows we will begin to explore what it might mean to embrace mediation as not only a necessary part of our worshiping lives together and with God but a positive one. Positive mediation appears in many ways in worship, but significantly in music.

THE MUSIC BETWEEN US: MUSIC AS MEDIA AND MEDIATION

Media of various forms are ubiquitous in musical performances and experiences. Printed music, microphones, amplification systems, amphitheaters, and even vocal technique (whether bel canto or Broadway) are media that function to shape these experiences. But how does music itself function as media? Does music mediate, and if so, what does it mediate, and how?

Musicologist Mia Nakamura writes about music as both a medium and as mediation. Music is a medium that also mediates relationships and meaning; this mediation could be compared to a letter or document that expresses or formalizes a relationship between people or groups. The written communication is a kind of mediation that transforms or establishes a relational dynamic, even while it is simultaneously a media object. Music works in much the same way.[13] Anthropologist and musicologist Georgina Born also writes about the mediated nature of music. She describes music as a "multiply-mediated, immaterial and material, fluid quasiobject, in which subjects and objects collide and intermingle." Music exists through "assemblages," or historically contextual constructions of meaning and practice "between musicians and instruments, composers and scores, listeners and sound systems."[14]

---

[12]De Witte, "Modes of Binding," 186.
[13]Mia Nakamura, "Music Sociology Meets Neuroscience," in *The Oxford Handbook of Music and the Body*, ed. Youn Kim and Sander L. Gilman (New York: Oxford University Press, 2018), 127.
[14]Georgina Born, "On Musical Mediation: Ontology, Technology and Creativity," *Twentieth-Century Music* 2, no. 1 (2005): 7.

I will discuss some of these concepts—assemblages, the historically situated relationships between music, culture, and technology—in what follows in order to make clear the importance of these categories for making sense of mediation in the church's music. In line with the methodology of this book, Born presents music "as a medium that destabilizes some of our most cherished dualisms concerning the separation not only of subject from object, but present from past, individual from collectivity, the authentic from the artificial, and production from reception."[15]

Mediation is often presented as a category diametrically opposed to immediacy or genuine experience. Patrick Valiquet writes about the sometimes confusing disconnect between popular vocabulary around mediation and its role in music. Valiquet says, "It is possible in principle to interpret all music as multiply mediated, and mediating.... Nevertheless, we still most often hear of mediation in discussions of musical assemblages where recording, transmission, or sound synthesis technologies play a central role." He notes that references to mediation in these contexts tend to interpret those expressions as "a break with or impediment to 'immediate', face-to-face communication."[16] Valiquet suggests that understanding mediations and technologies as barriers in musical communication falls short of grasping the significance of mediation. The media technologies that have not yet been erased for us still seem unsettling; however, arrangements of various technologies and mediations used in music throughout history have changed and shifted over the centuries. There is not one "original" or "pure" way of engaging with music without the use of media.

One helpful concept in discussing musical mediation is the category of an assemblage. This is a broader category in cultural theory used by thinkers across disciplines. Drawing on the work of Gilles Deleuze and Paul Rabinow, Born applies assemblage to music specifically and defines "a (musical) assemblage as a particular combination of mediations (sonic, discursive, visual, artefactual, technological, social, temporal) characteristic of a certain musical culture and historical period."[17] In the context of music, then, *assemblage*

---

[15]Born, "On Musical Mediation," 8.

[16]Patrick Valiquet, "A Managed Risk: Mediated Musicianships in a Networked Laptop Orchestra," *Contemporary Music Review* 37, no. 5-6 (2018): 647.

[17]Born, "On Musical Mediation," 8; Gilles Deleuze and Paul Bove, *Foucault*, trans. Sean Hand (Minneapolis: University of Minnesota Press, 1988); Paul Rabinow, *Anthropos Today: Reflections on Modern Equipment* (Princeton, NJ: Princeton University Press, 2009), 44-56.

refers to a cultural and technological way of arranging how music functions socially, economically, and philosophically. An assemblage is a set of mediations that shape what we believe music is and what values inform our practice of it. Born provides a number of examples to highlight the ways different assemblages have shaped and reshaped perceptions of music through different historical periods. Each culture and moment in time is likely to have a dominant form of musical assemblage.[18]

One major assemblage Born highlights, which continues to heavily influence music today, developed out of musical Romanticism in the 1800s. Born writes of the Romantic principle that "musical invention depended on the self-expression of the individual composer-genius, who must refuse to follow established rules or submit to external controls; and the arrival of a 'work-based practice' centred on the belief that musical works were perfectly formed, finished and 'untouchable', and transcended any particular performance." This cultural narration of music led to valuing precise notation, investing printed scores with a high degree of authority, carefully distinguishing which works were "original," and emphasizing the composer's original genius and intention with intellectual property rights.[19]

The romantic assemblage of a genius composer producing a perfect and inviolable musical work interacted with media technologies and performance practices and values around music to influence what was considered valuable and appropriate music making. This assemblage highlights the idea of media ecologies described by Tom Wagner (see the introduction). Various media are influenced by each other and by shifting norms of how each is used. This influence reveals what Born calls "two-way interrelations between music and social life." These assemblages become relatively stable structures of musical meaning, although they can shift over time. Born asserts, "Such stabilities of meaning can be repeatedly observed in music history, as powerful discourses or metaphors come to structure musical experience . . . conditioning future musical expressions and compositional practices." The Romantic assemblage is built around the "ontology of the musical work" and is hierarchical; "the composer-hero stands over the interpreter, conductor over instrumentalist,

---

[18]Born, "On Musical Mediation," 8.
[19]Born, "On Musical Mediation," 9-10.

interpreter over listener, just as the work ideal authorizes and supervises the score, which supervises performance, which supervises reception."[20]

This particular imagination about music's mediation (or lack thereof) emphasizes some forms and directions of mediation; the composer's genius is mediated through the written musical score, which is the closest access possible to "the music" itself. Individual performances, recordings, and the social realities of music are largely irrelevant to the "true" nature of the music. But this assemblage, or construction of what music is, does not apply in all circumstances.

Other genres and contexts of music have their own assemblages. We might describe multiple assemblages within various genres of worship music, incorporating differing relationships to the songwriter, to musical notation, and to particular performances. A hymn such as Martin Luther's "A Mighty Fortress Is Our God" carries with it narratives about its creation, paths of mediation, and norms around its performance. This assemblage is distinctly different from the constellation of cultural and theological narratives around a modern worship song described as being "a gift from God" to an individual songwriter or a charismatic chorus that arose spontaneously in a Spirit-filled worship gathering.

But even these assemblages are not constant across time. Whatever category of music is being described, historical and cultural context come into play. Born highlights how "electronic and digital technologies afford and enhance a dispersed and collaborative creativity." Whereas in previous permutations, recordings and notated music allowed for sharing musical ideas, digital media are transforming these processes: "With centrifugal force, and more easily than in its commodity forms, music is scattered, flung via the internet in near-real time from any point of creation and departure to any number of points of destination." Additionally, music mediated through digital media and the internet becomes exponentially more difficult to control by economic and copyright restrictions. Digitized music is hypermobile and tends toward an ongoing recirculation and recreation rather than an authoritative urtext.[21]

---

[20] Born, "On Musical Mediation," 13-14, 26-27.
[21] Born, "On Musical Mediation," 25.

The concept of musical assemblages highlights that "music's ontology and its mediation must be grasped as historical."[22] The ways we understand music's mediation are shifting, along with the rest of our world, as we move forward in the digital age. These mediations take discursive, material, and social forms; in other words, the ways music is talked about and understood, how music interacts with physical objects, and how music intersects with social structures are all forms of mediation. The internet affects all of these. Music's discursive mediations are accelerated and spread more widely than ever before through blogs, online reviews, discussion forums, and digital publication. The internet "stimulates an intensification, expansion and democratization of this discursivity, inciting participation and speeding up its production and circulation."[23] Significantly, the internet also has a profound effect on music's social mediation. Not only do existing cultural structures such as record labels, concerts, and festivals now exist as hybrid (both offline and online) realities, but new "natively digital social forms" are appearing (including communities gathered around artists and genres and mediated through social media), which then affect offline realities.[24] I will explore intersections between social media platforms and music in a later chapter.

Music is always a mediated phenomenon, the assemblages of this musical mediation are historically situated, and we are living through a major transition between conflicting assemblages. The place music will have in society, the ways we make and share music, and the meanings these mediations carry will all be in flux for the foreseeable future.

IMMEDIACY IN THE MIDDLE: A PHILOSOPHY OF MEDIATION

While church music scholars may argue that liturgy always involves mediation, and musicologists contend that music is always media and mediation, the philosophy around mediation is also significant to consider. This is because philosophical understandings of mediation can helpfully nuance and problematize our commonsense assumptions about what mediation is and

---

[22] Born, "On Musical Mediation," 34.
[23] Georgina Born and Christopher Haworth, "Music and Intermediality After the Internet: Aesthetics, Materialities and Social Forms," in *Music and Digital Media: A Planetary Anthropology*, ed. Georgina Born (London: UCL Press, 2022), 378.
[24] Born and Haworth, "Music and Intermediality," 381.

how it shapes our experiences of the world. The philosophy of mediation informs these conversations in other disciplines and carries many similar themes. In his article "Radical Mediation," Richard Grusin sets out to give an account of mediation that has utility in our historical moment. Grusin describes the importance of this endeavor, highlighting that this question "has become one of the central intellectual problems in the late twentieth and twenty-first centuries, in part because of the extraordinary acceleration of technology, the rampant proliferation of digital media technologies that sometimes goes under the name of 'mediatization.'"[25]

Given the rapid increase of digital media technologies, it is understandable that many conversations around mediation focus on these new cultural expressions. However, Grusin takes this concept of mediation a step further, seeking to highlight overarching themes of mediation that operate across all areas of life. He contends, "Mediation operates not just across communication, representation, or the arts, but is a fundamental process of human and nonhuman existence." He describes his position as advocating for "radical mediation" and offers it as a corrective to "dualistic" Western models of mediation. Grusin argues that media of all forms do not only communicate between separate objects or entities but transform all parties involved: "Mediations are always remediations, which change or translate experiences as well as relating or connecting them. . . . While radical empiricism insists on the reality of experienced relations, radical mediation also insists upon an immediacy that transforms, modulates, or disrupts experienced relations."[26]

It may sound counterintuitive, but Grusin's argument is that mediation touches all of life and that all of life is simultaneously immediate. "Radical mediation" is in contradiction to representationalism, or "the belief in the ontological distinction between representations and what they purport to represent." On a representationalist account, mediation comes between "already preformed, preexistent subjects or objects, actants or entities." This account describes mediation as a process connecting across a distance that would not otherwise allow understanding or interaction. Grusin points out that in the wake of post-Hegelian, Marxian philosophy, mediation and

---

[25] Richard Grusin, "Radical Mediation," *Critical Inquiry* 42, no. 1 (2015): 124.
[26] Grusin, "Radical Mediation," 125, 128.

immediacy are often placed in opposition to each other. Mediation in this frame is unavoidable but also distorts our experience of the world. Grusin summarizes how "in many traditional philosophical accounts we cannot experience the world directly or immediately because we cannot know the world without some form of mediation."[27]

Radical mediation pushes back against this understanding. Rather than mediation being simultaneously a necessary connector and an inevitable barrier between separate parties, Grusin offers an alternative account in which mediation is "the process, action, or event that generates or provides the conditions for the emergence of subjects and objects, for the individuation of entities within the world." In other words, mediation is necessary to and creates the space in which relationship occurs: "Mediation is not opposed to immediacy but rather is itself immediate. It names the immediacy of middleness in which we are already living and moving." On this account, humanity finds itself not on islands of experience irretrievably separated from reality and from others, but in the network of mediation's transformations and relations. Reality is in the middle, in the mediations, in our midst.[28]

Grusin critiques another concept related to mediation that is relevant to this research. This is "the logic of transparent immediacy," which suggests that "the medium erases itself so that there is an immediate subjective encounter with, or apprehension of, the object of mediation, or the real. . . . Transparent immediacy holds that the subject's contact with the real depends on the erasure of the medium, which correlates and thereby obscures the relationship between subject and world." This maps closely onto Ingalls's, Busman's, Steuernagel's, Klaver's, and Berger's accounts of worship music and liturgy. The church often feels compelled to attempt to erase, obscure, or ignore the reality and immediacy of mediation in an effort to achieve unmediated access to the divine. Unmediated access seems possible

---

[27] Grusin, "Radical Mediation," 129.
[28] Grusin, "Radical Mediation," 129. This account of radical mediation shares similarities with intersubjectivity. See also Pamela Cooper-White, "Intersubjectivity," in *Encyclopedia of Psychology and Religion*, ed. David A. Leeming (Boston: Springer, 2014), 882-86; Daniel Chandler and Rod Munday, *A Dictionary of Media and Communication* (Oxford: Oxford University Press, 2020), 452-53; Elizabeth H. Margulis et al., "Narratives Imagined in Response to Instrumental Music Reveal Culture-Bounded Intersubjectivity," *Proceedings of the National Academy of Sciences of the United States of America* 119, no. 4 (January 2022): e2110406119.

Mediation and Virtuality

only by the removal of media (specifically, media involving technologies that are relatively new and therefore not yet invisible). In contrast, Grusin suggests, "For radical mediation, all bodies (whether human or nonhuman) are fundamentally media and life itself is a form of mediation." Radical mediation does not remove the significance of media technologies and objects, however. Rather, it acknowledges, "There is no distance or perspective from which to see immediacy, from which immediacy could be made into something one could paint or draw or re-present, or something that needed mediation."[29]

Grusin writes, "The core of radical mediation is its immanence, immediacy itself . . . the embodied immediacy of the event of mediation." I suggest that radical mediation can be a productive focus for theological reflection, with implications for our musical and liturgical practices.

THE KINGDOM OF GOD IS IN YOUR MIDST: MEDITATIONS ON MEDIATION

If all of life is mediated, and mediation radically overlaps and interpenetrates human relationships, where does this leave human experiences of God in worship? The reality that even these most foundational spiritual experiences always involve media and mediation may be disconcerting to some. However, the good news is that even—and perhaps especially—through our experiences of mediation, God is able and chooses to reach us, and invites us to encounter God. In fact, mediation is better understood as presenting opportunities for connection with others and with God, not obstacles to immediacy in relationship.

When asked about the significance of mediation and desires for immediacy in faith, Heidi Campbell immediately resonated with the question. As a scholar of digital religion, she is familiar with the anxieties many Christians experience around media and has spent time reflecting on the implications of various media on faith practices. Campbell claims that, rather than being in conflict with Christian thought and tradition, mediation allowing for connection and community across distance has been a part of the church since its beginning: "Our tradition and our faith has always been mediated

---

[29]Grusin, "Radical Mediation," 130, 132.

because we have the Bible. The Word of God has been mediated through all these generations." She describes Paul as "the first virtual apostle or theologian," and the epistles written to early churches as an example of religious community mediated across distance. She also highlights familiar language about the "global body of Christ," which includes those we cannot see or touch.[30]

The Christian faith always included mediation through oral tradition and shared stories that were eventually compiled into the biblical canon. Not only that, but our patterned practices of worship and the ways we gather are mediated as well. Pete Phillips offers these reflections on the mediations inherent in worship:

> And so church is always mediated. Everything is mediated, you know. . . . The fact [is] that we live in a world with increasing amounts of media engagement. But historically it's always been mediated as well. The temple was a media space. The high places were media spaces. The burning bush was a media space. A bush was burning, and God spoke out of it. That's pretty high-level mediation. Moses going into the tabernacle and coming out glowing is a mediation. The tabernacle itself, again, mediated space, the temple mediated through architecture, through laws, through smells, through music, through . . . everything. . . . So often we forget about technology because it's been with us so long. It just becomes part and parcel of everything else. And so we regard church buildings not as being technology. We regard them as simply the natural place to do worship. And so . . . because we regard them as natural spaces, they're "unmediated."[31]

The technologies we have become accustomed to fade from our awareness, becoming invisible to us, and we forget their mediations. But just as our frequent lack of awareness of God's presence does not negate that presence, our forgetting the ubiquity of media does not erase its existence. We are responsible for the media we use, new and old, all of which have potential both for facilitating immediate encounters in relationship and for erecting barriers of hierarchy and exclusion. When I interviewed Phillips, he talked about the power structures inherent in how many churches were built in England—everything from seating arrangements that privilege the rich and push the

---

[30]Heidi A. Campbell, interview by author, Zoom, January 20, 2023.
[31]Peter Phillips interview by author, Zoom, March 1, 2023.

Mediation and Virtuality

poor to stand in the back, to pews that are owned by influential people, to medieval rood screens that exclude laity from holy places.[32]

Phillips argues that the constant presence of technology and mediation throughout the history of Christianity and Judaism is not a problem to be solved to reach God but is an expression of God's nature that God's image-bearers also carry. For Phillips, the advent of digital technology and media is simply one more expression of the historical reality of media, with parallel opportunities and cautions to those that came before. He claims, "Nothing has been without technology," referencing God's speaking the earth into being as a use of the technology of language. Phillips describes God as "a technologist" who invites humans to use our skills with technology, citing Jesus of Nazareth's profession as a carpenter or builder, Noah's building the ark, and Bezalel and Oholiab's commissioning to decorate the tabernacle, among many other examples in Scripture. Phillips concludes, "Worship has always been technologized to some extent." Given this reality, Phillips finds a rejection of digital technology to be somewhat odd.

On Phillips's account, God has always worked through technology and media. God invites mediated encounter while also removing barriers to relationship through those mediations. Mediation can be a positive expression of relationship, not only an obstacle. Just as we have seen throughout the church's history, it *is* possible for mediations to impose unjust barriers to encounter with God. This potential is still present in digital mediations, and the church is called to make use of them in ways that are honoring to God and to God's creation and image-bearers. However, digital media do not carry more inherent potential for evil, or less for good, than a church building, a pew, or a book.

If we find ourselves in the middle of radical mediation, as Grusin suggests, it is fitting that Jesus is our mediator with God. Christ's mediation can be understood to break down the division between human and divine, within the being of the Son. The mediation of God *is* the immediacy of God, and God's relationship with creation is mediated within that creation, just as God rested within creation on the seventh day. "In [God] we live and move and have our being" (Acts 17:28). Christ is not a vanishing mediator who is erased

---

[32]Phillips, interview.

so that we can have access to God that would be blocked by mediation. Instead, the mediation of Jesus the Son experienced through the immediacy of the Holy Spirit and the community of faith *is* our experience of God's reality.

Just as there is no unmediated experience of the world, there is no unmediated worship, and there is no unmediated experience of God. Jesus is our mediator in relating to God, our great high priest. The immediacy of our relationship with God is heightened by the fact of Jesus' mediation, as fully God and fully human. When we pray to God the Father, we pray as those who were taught by Jesus to pray, "Our Father." When we experience the working of the Holy Spirit, we do so as those to whom Jesus has promised the Spirit from the Father. When we trust in Jesus as our faithful Savior, we do so through the mediation of our religious traditions, imaginations, texts, physical and ideological cultures, and across space and time.

What might the church do with this vision of divine mediation? Christians ought to be careful of either erasing mediators (those technologies that have become invisible, from hymns to hermeneutics) or claiming too confidently that because mediation is taking place, those experiences are illegitimate or unreal. Instead, we can come to all of our experiences, whether we are able to ignore the multiple mediations constantly at play or not, with an openness to the presence of the God who is always with us. The task of leading worship calls ministers to direct their own attention toward that presence, and to model and invite others to do the same, within our own radically mediated contexts.

THE FOURTH BINARY: VIRTUAL VERSUS REAL

It has become commonplace in American Christian church circles to refer to "virtual gatherings," "virtual worship," or "virtual community." We say we will meet "virtually" rather than "in person" for this or that event. But what do we mean by *virtual*, and what implications does this have for what we consider real, significant, and meaningful in our shared lives? Are books, posted signs, written letters, telephones, newspapers, email, and visual or musical art "virtual" or "real"? And what do we make of virtual reality, which seems to claim a blending of these two categories we often perceive as diametrically opposed? Is this new technology a threat to our growth in Christlike character, something that will malform us and isolate us? Or might it offer new opportunities for connection, inclusion, and even moral formation?

Mediation and Virtuality

In what follows I will answer these questions by exploring the concept of virtuality from several angles. I will begin by summarizing some of the work of Heidi A. Campbell and Wendi Bellar on the history of research and terminology around digital, online, or virtual media, interactions, and communities. This will lead, second, to a discussion of virtual reality, perspective taking in virtual environments and video games, and the formative moral potential of these media. Third, I will draw on insights from interviews from a pastor in virtual reality spaces and an ethnomusicologist studying virtual concerts to explore interactions between virtual reality and musical and ritual experiences. Finally, I will offer some guiding thoughts and questions about the significance of virtuality and reality as we move forward in discerning what the future of the church's worship and community practices might look like.

DIGITAL RELIGION AND THE VIRTUAL

In their book *Digital Religion: The Basics*, Heidi A. Campbell and Wendi Bellar describe the changing landscape of religion and the internet over the past four decades. They note that in the 1980s, people were already finding ways to transfer religious practices online via internet technologies. These experiments continued through the 1990s, when religious spaces were springing up online, including cyberchurches and prayer and meditation groups mediated through discussion boards and email lists.[33]

Terminology around this new technology has been in flux through the decades. Campbell and Bellar note that at the end of the twentieth century, *internet* and *cyberspace* were used synonymously. *Cyberspace* was envisioned in the popular imagination as "a unique kind of space, one very different and disconnected from people's 'real' life."[34] There were religious expressions online even during this period, but they were commonly understood as something separate and different from "real" religion.

These online religious expressions, understood as distinct and disconnected from offline rituals, came to be viewed as something of a threat. In the early 2000s, some religious leaders became concerned that people engaging with online faith communities were challenging established structures and

---

[33]Heidi A. Campbell and Wendi Bellar, *Digital Religion: The Basics* (London: Routledge, 2022), 1-2.
[34]Campbell and Bellar, *Digital Religion*, 2.

houses of worship. This growing dimension of religious practice online seemed to be undermining existing religious authority.[35] These new communication technologies provided opportunities for people to access and participate in religion in different ways. These mediated expressions seemed to portend a restructuring of institutional power and were therefore suspect.

As the first decade of the twenty-first century continued, there was an explosion of religious websites. The arrival of social media platforms such as Facebook and Twitter invited new forms of online religion. As this experimentation accelerated, the scholarly discourse shifted away from discussing *cyber-religion* toward *virtual religion*, echoing "ideas of virtual worlds, such as Second Life or online gaming platforms, which did not have an offline counterpart." However, before 2010, this terminology was already coming under scrutiny. Internet researchers began to realize that *virtual* was growing to be associated with virtual reality technology. Campbell and Bellar note that the "term virtual was used to refer to technologically created spaces or computer-simulated experiences. Calling something virtual became a way to distinguish online spaces from the 'real world,' where authentic community and religion were found." Describing religion as virtual at this time implied that it was "somehow incomplete or a false form." The divide between online and offline communities and rituals has continued to be negotiated and debated, but the reality of the virtual has become more and more accepted as these technologies become more integrated into our lives: "Scholars generally recognize that as the Internet and digital media increasingly are used to build, maintain, and support community relationships in contemporary culture, the online and offline expressions of the community are increasingly connected and overlapping rather than distinctly different."[36]

Researchers began to distinguish between traditional religious expressions brought online and new ritual expressions native to digital media. It also became clearer during this time that online religion was "empowering its members to create new rituals, bypass traditional systems of authority ... [and] transcend normal limits of time, space, and the body online."[37]

---

[35]Campbell and Bellar, *Digital Religion*, 2.
[36]Campbell and Bellar, *Digital Religion*, 3-4, 21.
[37]Campbell and Bellar, *Digital Religion*, 3-4.

In the 2010s, the field of digital religion studies was becoming more established, as were online expressions of religion. It became clear to scholars that the internet was a complex and multifaceted phenomenon and that accompanying digital technologies were far more integrated with "real" life than separate from it. This trajectory has continued, leading Campbell and Bellar to conclude, "Religion, as it is practiced online, mirrors changes long at work within broader culture impacting how religion is conceived and acted out in contemporary society." These changes include a shift in how people experience community (as less tied to geographical location and physical institutions, and more as a network of social relationships) and the integration of digital media in every aspect of life, from work, to education, to family.[38] Campbell and Bellar summarize these changes and offer the thought-provoking observation that all of our relationships are occasionally mediated, as digital media have become significant parts of our daily lives. Many experiences of community exist within this mediated context. As we will see in chapter four, the transformation of our daily lives and relationships to include digital media was heightened and highlighted during the Covid-19 pandemic.

When I asked Campbell to elaborate on the popular distinction between the virtual and the real, she offered further comments, noting that from 1990 to the mid-2000s, the distinction of virtual versus real was popular, but it has come to be understood as a false dichotomy and an unhelpful framing. Campbell went on to note that the word *virtual* has associations with virtual reality. This was once a "kind of science fiction dream" but in the past few years has become a real, practical technology. According to Campbell, arguments against using (recent) technology in the church "are all based on that assumption that . . . the offline is real and it's perfect, and the online is flawed, and it's going to lead you into problematic directions." However, the pandemic has revealed that even our offline ideals may be flawed. Campbell remarks that this realization makes many churches uncomfortable and they have tended to "quickly slip that under the rug." At the same time, she notes that there are many more conversations happening around these issues now than before.[39]

---

[38]Campbell and Bellar, *Digital Religion*, 4, 7, 22.
[39]Campbell, interview.

The terminology used to describe digital religion has shifted over the past four decades, as have the meanings and implications of those terms. From *cyber-religion* to *virtual religion* to *digital religion*, both ordinary people and scholars have continued to experience and negotiate what it means to engage with new technologies and the ways they are interacting with and transforming the world around us. As the virtual becomes more fully integrated with the "real" world, we will need to keep learning and exploring what opportunities and pitfalls face the church of the future.

IT'S NO GAME: VIRTUAL REALITY AND REAL VIRTUE

A primary concern in discerning the role of digital media and virtual experiences in Christian worship is whether these technologies have the potential to serve the goal of discipleship. Can online interactions have any formative moral impact? Does virtual reality have any bearing on our real lives? This section will explore insights from research around virtual reality and video games to argue that moral formation is indeed possible using digital media.

In his 2021 chapter "Virtual Embodiment and Embodied Cognition: Effect of Virtual Reality Perspective Taking Tasks on Empathy and Prejudice," Fernanda Herrera explores the significance of virtual reality experiences. He acknowledges at the outset that these new technologies represent a departure from human experience up to this point. Humans historically moved through and understood the world by means of our direct senses and physical presence. A significant departure from this came with written language and symbols, which enabled us to learn and communicate regardless of direct physical presence (reading this book is one example). In the twenty-first century, this landscape has changed again: "Now, with the availability of virtual reality (VR) technology, for the first time in our history we are able to embody different kinds of bodies and explore new virtual environments with our own physical bodies."[40] This newness is part of the challenge with which American church leaders are contending. The church has experienced technological shifts in the past; at the same time, being human in society does not

---

[40] Fernanda Herrera, "Virtual Embodiment and Embodied Cognition: Effect of Virtual Reality Perspective Taking Tasks on Empathy and Prejudice," in *A Multidisciplinary Approach to Embodiment: Understanding Human Being*, ed. Nancy Kimberly Dess (New York: Routledge, 2021), 127.

mean the same things it used to, nor does it involve the same practices and media it did before.

At the turn of the century, the transition into the digital revolution was just beginning. Reflections on the nature and potential of virtual reality from this period offer a helpful perspective today. In his 1999 book *Digital Sensations: Space, Identity, and Embodiment in Virtual Reality*, Ken Hillis writes about the impact of what he calls "virtual environments" on our conception of space and the relationships mediated by shared space. Hillis contends that Western thought carries two distinct understandings of communication. Respectively, these conceive of communication as either "transmission of information through space" or "communication as ritual—the maintenance of society in time through representation of shared beliefs among people brought together in one place." In this second understanding, shared space is crucial as a "middle ground drawing together the disparate elements into communication."[41]

In his description of virtual environments, Hillis argues that both understandings of communication—as transmission through space and as place-bound ritual—come together, such that "the act of transmission itself becomes an ersatz place and constitutes a ritual act or performance." This echoes Grusin's argument for understanding mediation as a space in the middle where we experience immediate encounter. For Hillis, virtual environments "merge absolute and relational concepts of space." Hillis argues, "Social relations, agency, and meanings take place in, and are influenced by, space and how it is used." The space or atmosphere in which relations occur is a medium permitting the flow of information. These spaces, atmospheres, or media allow us to share experiences, ritual acts, and communal identity; in Hillis's words, "We give places meaning, and in return they offer us existential support." Hillis claims that virtual reality facilitates something called telepresence. *Telepresence* refers to "the experience of presence in an environment by means of a communication medium."[42] Virtual environments become mediated spaces that allow for two kinds of communication: both transmission across geographical distance and ritual in shared place.

---

[41] Ken Hillis, *Digital Sensations: Space, Identity, and Embodiment in Virtual Reality*, Electronic Mediations 1 (Minneapolis: University of Minnesota Press, 1999), 62.
[42] Hillis, *Digital Sensations*, 62, 77-78, 82, 182.

However, this early understanding of the potential of virtual reality did not find expression in wide popular adoption and experimentation. The technology involved was expensive and unwieldy, and therefore did not become broadly available. Writing in 2021, Fernanda Herrera notes that it was not until 2015 that virtual reality devices (such as the Oculus Quest, Google Daydream, VIVE PRO, and Lenovo Explorer) became commercially accessible. Prior to that, the technology was not advanced, efficient, or affordable enough to gain a popular audience. But these technologies are not only used for entertainment. Herrera offers a study of virtual reality's application for educational and therapeutic purposes. Herrera notes some reasons virtual reality is suited to this use case: "Some of the unique affordances of [virtual reality] systems are their ability to immerse users in virtual environments, allow them to embody different kinds of avatars, and elicit feelings of presence (i.e., the user's subjective feeling of being inside the virtual environment)."[43] These affordances allow for virtual reality to be an effective tool for training the emotional and physical responses of individuals in a variety of challenging situations. Put another way, virtual reality has the potential to shape real virtue.

One way the formative potential of virtual reality has been researched is through "virtual reality perspective taking" tasks. This research uses the unique affordances of virtual reality to explore how the technology can be used to "reduce prejudice and bias, increase understanding and empathy, lead to prosocial behaviors, and increase charitable donations." This is accomplished through completing tasks that involve embodying the perspective of someone with different experiences or identities from oneself in virtual reality. Herrera also notes, "Empirical evidence suggests that [virtual reality perspective taking] tasks can increase empathy for a myriad of social targets, including the elderly, people with schizophrenia, the homeless, individuals diagnosed with autism and children."[44]

It is possible to perform perspective-taking tasks without virtual reality. However, it seems that the technology is particularly effective. Herrera describes the impact that embodying a virtual avatar can have on a person's self-perception and behavior, saying, "The type of avatar users embody can impact self-perception, attitudes, and behavior both inside and outside the

---

[43]Herrera, "Virtual Embodiment and Embodied Cognition," 128.
[44]Herrera, "Virtual Embodiment and Embodied Cognition," 128.

virtual environment." He describes how users asked to perform a negotiation task in a virtual environment behaved differently based on their avatar. Users who embodied taller avatars were more confident and less likely to accept unfair offers than those across from them who were inhabiting shorter avatars in the virtual space. These shifts in behavior also persisted once the individuals had left the virtual environment, whether the person was shorter or taller in the physical world.[45] Herrera names this as an expression of the "body ownership illusion," which occurs when a person believes something is a part of them and experiences physical sensations through it. The body ownership illusion has been demonstrated in experiments with a rubber arm, in which one of the participant's hands is hidden from view. It is then replaced with the false limb, and through synchronized stimuli the participant is conditioned to believe the fake hand is their own.[46]

A similar phenomenon happens with virtual bodies within virtual reality. The avatar is integrated as part of the user's body schema (see chapter two) and at least momentarily becomes significant to their experience of the world. Herrera contends that body ownership illusions are not only escapist fantasies. Rather, they can "reshape social cognition ... mitigate stereotypes and reduce implicit racial biases when participants embody avatars that look like outgroup members." Several studies have shown reduced negative stereotyping and increased empathy through this effect.[47]

Whatever the combination of these factors that leads to the positive outcomes measured in virtual reality perspective-taking tasks, Herrera contends that this technology is particularly effective. He argues that, while traditional perspective-taking tasks depend on imagination, virtual reality perspective-taking tasks provide a more visceral, embodied experience. Users' physical reactions are much closer to what they would be if they were in that actual circumstance: "[Virtual reality perspective taking] tasks thus activate the same sensory, somatic, and motor states that would be activated if the experience was happening to the user in real life," allowing for "the interaction of both cognitive and whole-body states." Herrera concludes that this affordance of

---

[45]Herrera, "Virtual Embodiment and Embodied Cognition," 129.
[46]Marieke Rohde, Massimiliano Di Luca, and Marc O. Ernst, "The Rubber Hand Illusion: Feeling of Ownership and Proprioceptive Drift Do Not Go Hand in Hand," *PloS One* 6, no. 6 (2011): e21659.
[47]Herrera, "Virtual Embodiment and Embodied Cognition," 129-30.

virtual reality allows users to experience greater empathy and understanding of people different from themselves.[48] This technology is still relatively new and is just beginning to gain greater traction and broad adoption and accessibility. It seems possible, however, that it may provide new formative opportunities for people to learn to love their neighbors as themselves.

While Herrera's research is focused on uses of virtual reality outside typical entertainment applications, there are reasons to consider the moral implications of video games as well. As more of our society operates through digital media, we will continue to find productive insights in examining video games. Benjamin J. Chicka's recent book, *Playing as Others: Theology and Ethical Responsibility in Video Games*, presents a case for reflecting on the presence of God and human responsibility to others through this medium.[49] A primary focus of Chicka's argument is closely related to Herrera's discussion of virtual reality as a method of building empathy and decreasing prejudice. Chicka traces the trajectory of the video game industry as it has moved toward including and representing greater diversity. As studios developing games became more diverse and the characters depicted in their games did as well, more opportunities for this perspective taking emerged. Gamers encountered "virtual others they may be segregated from in daily life, others they might even actively reject in society." These new games mediated virtual encounters that the physical and cultural contours of our society might preclude, and even invited players to embody identities quite different from their own in a uniquely interactive medium. They also provided representation for marginalized groups in empowering ways. Chicka concludes that this experience "gives people the courage to be themselves in the world in the face of adversity" or can provide "opportunities to learn about the importance of embracing the other, and to carry that lesson into the real world."[50]

Chicka's account resonates strongly with the goals of virtual reality perspective-taking tasks. Many people often experience digital and social media as polarizing and dehumanizing, in which the particularity and dignity of the "others" they encounter through the internet are erased or even harmed.

---

[48] Herrera, "Virtual Embodiment and Embodied Cognition," 130-31.
[49] Benjamin J. Chicka, *Playing as Others: Theology and Ethical Responsibility in Video Games* (Waco, TX: Baylor University Press, 2021), 15.
[50] Chicka, *Playing as Others*, 17.

Mediation and Virtuality

Similarly, virtual reality and video games could certainly be used to harmful ends. However, this is not the only way for digital technologies to be used, and there are redemptive potentialities as well.

Chicka argues that the crisis of moral responsibility to the other can be understood as recognizing what Emmanuel Lévinas terms the "face" of the other.[51] Nathan Myrick applies Lévinas's logic to church music in *Music for Others: Care, Justice, and Relational Ethics in Christian Music*. Myrick summarizes Lévinas's significance for this field, writing, "The foundation of ethics is to care for others because of the ontology of human relationships; a self becomes essential because of the presence of an other."[52] He goes on to contend,

> Any activity of music involves others, whether encountered through physical presence or through such virtual means as history, memory, or imagination. Because of this relational aspect, ethical responsibilities should not be suspended in any musical endeavor. Instead, the activity of listening to and performing music with others causes us to enter into relational responsibility with them.[53]

To the virtual means Myrick describes, we might add those means involving digital technologies. Entering into relational responsibility with others, which Lévinas, Chicka, and Myrick connect to the face of the other, is possible through music and even through digital technology.

In positive face-to-face encounters, we experience an ethical call to the wholeness, integrity, and flourishing of the human life we behold. Chicka argues that humanity has fallen short in recognizing the ethical call that is still present in mediated encounters. He writes, "In a world increasingly connected virtually rather than in-person, realizing the ethical call from the virtual face of the other is of crucial importance for our future on this fragile planet."[54] What is essential in the face-to-face encounter and the ethical demands placed on us in relationship is not the fact of light bouncing off skin into our eyes (which is a form of mediation in itself). Rather, the quality

---

[51] Emmanuel Lévinas, *Otherwise than Being, or, Beyond Essence* (Pittsburgh: Duquesne University Press, 1998).
[52] Nathan Myrick, *Music for Others: Care, Justice, and Relational Ethics in Christian Music* (London: Oxford University Press, 2021), 106.
[53] Myrick, *Music for Others*, 95-96.
[54] Chicka, *Playing as Others*, 21.

and moral significance of a face-to-face encounter is possible even in mediated environments. The face of the other is not merely a physical experience, and physical encounter is not a precondition for entering into this kind of ethical relationship.[55]

Our failure to appreciate the face of the other through digital and virtual means is just that—a failure, largely born of our inexperience with these new technologies. Rather than giving up on the potential of these technologies to facilitate meaningful connections and relationships, we can explore how they might allow for transformative moral commitment that can work counter-culturally against isolation and an exploitative attention economy.

VIRTUAL REALITY MUSIC AND LITURGY

If it is possible for virtual reality to have positive moral impacts and to summon us to the ethical imperative of care for others, what does this mean for music? How do people experience music in virtual environments? What are some of the characteristics of current expressions of Christian liturgies in virtual environments, and what are some potential directions it might take in the future? Two major insights emerged from interviews with DJ Soto, a virtual reality pastor, and Laryssa Whittaker, an ethnomusicologist who studies virtual concerts. The first of these is the social and experimental motivations central to virtual reality users' experience. The second is the potential for immersive experiences that show promise for allowing people in a variety of circumstances to encounter music in new ways.

Virtual reality has become a much more accessible and widely used technology since 2016. One important theme that has emerged during this time is how significant the social aspect is to people who use virtual reality. Soto shared with me his reflections on the historical trajectory of early popular virtual reality and virtual reality church. He notes that, while people assume virtual reality church is filled with Millennials or "the younger gamer crowd," these are not the primary demographics that first adopted the technology. Soto describes how previously, virtual reality technology was quite new and prohibitively expensive for some. People over forty with more access to disposable income were able to spend the money (Soto estimates $2,000) to get

---

[55]Chicka, *Playing as Others*, 101.

into virtual reality in its early days (prices have continued to drop in the years since). Rather than young gamers, Soto first saw an influx of a different demographic with their own priorities, who logged into virtual spaces in search of social connections. These early adopters indicated what would become a primary driver of virtual reality use in the years since. Soto articulates this draw to virtual reality, saying, "It's about the social connections and interactions that we have never had like that. . . . It's the first time in history where we're having these face-to-face interactions, avatar to avatar, in these immersive worlds."[56]

Virtual reality is often perceived as an antisocial, isolating technology, encouraging people to retreat into escapist virtual worlds away from human connection in the real world. However, this is the opposite of what Soto and Whittaker describe from their experience and research. Whittaker describes the essentially social nature of virtual reality for many participants, saying, "Largely, people are not that interested in using it on its own, ever, in any context." Whittaker was involved in a longitudinal study of eighty people using virtual reality, and while some engaged with virtual reality for relaxation and recreation, the study found that many people found the still-new technology cumbersome enough that it did not seem worthwhile for these purposes. Whittaker notes the "frictions" of using virtual reality at home, whether keeping the device charged or finding a large enough space to move around in, reduced motivation for study participants to use it. She suggests that using virtual reality on its own was not rewarding enough for how much mental energy it took.

However, where many people did find virtual reality rewarding was in sharing social connections. Whittaker narrates how "they had really creative ways of getting social in [virtual reality], even on things that weren't intended to be social. . . . They would Chromecast the headsets to the TV, so that everybody could watch while one person's in the headset. . . . Fascinating stuff about turn taking and watching each other play and how much fun that was for people was hilarious, actually." Whittaker continues to wonder whether a current barrier to broader virtual reality adoption might be industry fixation on the technology as something an individual uses alone. Users seemed far

---

[56] DJ Soto, interview by author, Zoom, January 13, 2023.

more interested in social applications; Whittaker suggests that as virtual reality becomes "more accessible, [more] democratized . . . then I think we might finally see some uptake in adoption because people aren't that keen to just sit around and do it by themselves."[57]

As with previous technological innovations (such as the printing press, radio, and television), new technologies often face challenges to their early integration into existing ways of life. As the technology continues to develop and become more convenient and more affordable, virtual reality may become a more significant part of society, with greater ease of use and fewer barriers to engaging with it. But so far, these experts are observing an important trend toward social engagement using the technology.

Whittaker expands on the second trend observed in virtual music: the potential for new and different kinds of musical experiences that both met particular needs and opened new creative possibilities. Here she notes the motivations behind virtual concert attendance in the wake of the Covid-19 pandemic's profound disruption of live music performances:

> People saw it as a time to experiment with new artists, new forms of music that they never would have engaged with before. People were talking again during Covid about just the opportunity to have some kind of live experience, a reasonable facsimile of a live experience. To have that sense of, there is a world out there, there are other people doing things, and we're all listening to this together. And to some extent, the numbers initially are looking like, yeah, that's dropped off since Covid has ended, but things have not gone back to pre-Covid levels, and I don't know that they will. People aren't going to live events as much as they did before Covid.[58]

Virtual reality concerts provided opportunities to engage with live music while minimizing health risks. Online concert attendance is also very convenient for many, even though it does not provide quite the same communal, physical, haptic experience in a shared physical space. But Whittaker noted other benefits as well that are not offered by traditional concert attendance. Virtual concert attendees felt a greater degree of access to artists. They wanted to be able to engage with the artists, chat with them, and make

---

[57]Laryssa Whittaker, interview by author, Zoom, April 18, 2023.
[58]Whittaker, interview.

Mediation and Virtuality

requests or ask questions; these interactions are more possible in the new virtual medium.[59]

Virtual reality concerts limit some aspects of interaction but also open up new avenues for connection between performers and audiences, and among audience members. Whittaker describes how virtual reality offered opportunities to avoid negative experiences of concerts, voicing the concerns of these concertgoers. These included wanting to be able to see clearly without others in front blocking their view, disliking people around them being disruptive or noisy, not wanting to be subjected to an overly loud or distorted sound system they could not control, mitigating feelings of agoraphobia, and even simply acknowledging that other concertgoers could be irritating in ways that virtual reality spaces mitigate. Whittaker notes a tension present between the positive aspects of social experience at a concert and the numerous ways other people can negatively affect the experiences of others. She names the impulse to control some of these undesirable elements of a concert being a major theme coming out of her research thus far.[60]

Virtual reality concerts, then, are a space for people to experiment with new kinds of music, new artists, and new experiences. They also provide opportunities for limiting the negative aspects of live music attendance and open new avenues of interaction with artists and between audience members.

Church music in virtual reality also has the potential for new expressions, even as there are some limitations from the current state of the technology. Soto described the form that music has taken in worship within virtual reality church to this point. This sometimes includes live performances, in which an individual plays an instrument and sings from their home, with the audio being picked up in the virtual reality space. Soto noted that these performances, whether with guitar or piano, have been very engaging. They have also sometimes used worship videos. Soto acknowledges that, at this early stage, the musical elements of virtual reality church are not as robust as those in some physical church spaces. This is due in part to the limitations imposed by the lag on the platform, which creates challenges combining multiple musicians. Bands and choirs aren't yet practical due to the desync over the online connection.

---

[59]Whittaker, interview.
[60]Whittaker, interview.

Soto is confident that this issue will be solved eventually but also notes that the music still functions in a similar way: "It's still really good, by the way. It's not like there's some deficiency. You see avatars raising their hand during worship time, right? And so you see that it's evoking the emotion. You can look across the metaverse church and see people's reaction, people swaying, people like nodding their head, you know. So there is connection at a basic level."[61] Soto's description represents the early stages of worship in virtual reality; as Soto mentions, there are ways that the technology can be developed further. Some of the limitations of the technology do place constraints on what can be done currently. But Soto also believes there are unique opportunities for musical worship in virtual reality:

> So as we compare them, [virtual reality worship] feels a little sub to the physical, but here's where the potential is, and that's just us catching up to where the technology is. . . . We haven't done this, but we're going to very soon, let's say there's a worship song about heaven and then the ground beneath you turns into clouds. Light starts forming all around you. Let's say there's an aspect of . . . a storm at sea. All of a sudden a boat envelops you, right? And then there's water coming down. And so the potential of worship, while we're not there yet, is really going to be very interesting when it comes to the metaverse, because it's not going to be just about the song and the words from a just audible [experience]. Now you're going to experience it, now you're going to see it. The song is going to take on a whole new life. It's going to go to a whole other level.[62]

Soto describes the potential implications of these developments, which can be seen in platforms creating immersive music videos. While previous experiences of recorded music have been mediated through the radio or music videos, whether on television or YouTube, new expressions are appearing in which a viewer is transported into a three-dimensional environment with surround sound. Soto suggests, "That's where worship will go soon, probably sooner than later. . . . We're not there yet, and I know when we do get there, it's just going to take [virtual reality church] to a whole other level because it's just going to be so unique. People have never been able to experience worship like this."[63]

---

[61] Soto, interview.
[62] Soto, interview.
[63] Soto, interview.

These kinds of virtual worship experiences will raise many further questions for the church as technology and culture continue to move forward. Soto is still dreaming of what might be possible, but the technology is likely ready for greater expressions of creativity and artistry in virtual liturgies. Whether and how this technology is appropriately used in a given context will be matters of discernment and ongoing theological reflection, as it was for the church at every previous technological revolution. The music of the church may not yet be at this point, but these experimental performances and concerts are already appearing in other settings.

Many church leaders will likely have instinctive negative reactions to these ideas and possibilities. Both our prereflective responses and our theological reflections will likely be challenged as technology and its use in the church continue to shift. The dichotomies named in this research will likely loom large in theological conversations as the church encounters these new realities. But if virtual experiences can lead to personal and moral transformation, the church will need to ask difficult and layered questions about how it will navigate both the unfounded anxieties about new technology and the genuine problems that are present in this revolutionary landscape.

WHERE DOES CHURCH GO FROM HERE?

Given the difficulties inherent in understanding and navigating new experiences and unfamiliar technologies, how can the church be prepared to move forward? Taking a nondualistic understanding of the virtual/real spectrum can help us to experience the material and spiritual as overlapping and interpenetrating one another. Christian scholars and practitioners can take a posture of curiosity, exploring what may be possible in this new technological era while also being aware of the malforming narratives and economies that may pull these technologies toward goals other than the flourishing of creation and worship of the Creator. A productive way forward will move through openness to new realities into a countercultural vision and witness that dignifies human lives and forms our communities toward greater virtue. If we reject the new out of hand without understanding, we will miss significant opportunities. At the same time, we will do well to be aware of forces and structures that may misdirect our efforts, such as economies that thrive on monetized distraction and toxic polarization.

Just as the church has been affected variously by the printing press, the radio, and the television, these revolutionary new digital and online technologies will require a reshaping of the church's vision of its interaction with the world. The church cannot afford to ignore or shut down this important sphere of human culture and community in the twenty-first century. Instead, Christian leaders and communities will be forced to grapple with the ways that online and offline realities continue to intermingle more and more. Familiar structures such as membership in local religious organizations now overlap and interact with online websites, communities, and experiences to fulfill social needs and shape individual and group identities. Online religious practice serves "as an extension of [digital media users'] conventional religious practice and spiritual meaning-making."[64] People no longer draw on only the offline or only the online for understanding their spirituality and religious life; both are unavoidably combined.

---

[64]Campbell and Bellar, *Digital Religion*, 65.

Hybridity and Church Music

IN THE PREVIOUS TWO CHAPTERS I have engaged with four categories that American Christians often perceive as being dichotomies that make online worship practices untenable. Online worship is often cast in terms of being passive rather than active, as disembodied rather than embodied, as mediated rather than unmediated, and as virtual rather than real. I have argued that these dichotomies are reductive and do not represent the actual limits and latent potential of digitally mediated religion. New media do not necessarily represent a defiling or diluting force on the witness and worship of the church. At the same time, it is not enough to say that because of these arguments (which some may find more or less compelling) American churches should unquestioningly embrace digital religious practice in its most common current forms. I suggest that the way forward for churches is not to resist the digital revolution but to engage with it while simultaneously discerning what values and virtues will shape our best expressions of faith and humanity in a world that increasingly integrates online and offline realities seamlessly.

To begin, I will explore the concept of hybridity between online and offline experiences and practices. Later in this chapter, I will focus on the philosophy of church music, seeking to explore the purposes of our musicking. This exploration will not offer a single prescriptive way for all churches to describe what the importance and function of church music is; rather, it will present a variety of values, recognizing that each context will include and prioritize different values. Each church or faith community can apply these principles according to their own theological emphases and situation. Discerning a philosophy of church music will help to guide contextual decisions about how online media can be helpfully used within the church's worship. I also include a discussion of insights we can glean from online and hybrid worship during the early stages of the Covid-19 pandemic, and a set of potential criteria for evaluating online practices of music and community.

There is not a single right way for churches to respond to online digital community and the hybrid realities of life in the twenty-first century. However, there are principles that can help us faithfully respond to the shifting landscapes around us and guide us toward cultivating practices that are participatory, transformative, appropriate to the medium being used, and centered on God. This chapter and the next will focus particularly on how the church can move forward in discerning what its musical life might look like in its online and offline, hybrid future.

INTEGRATED FAITH IN A HYBRID WORLD

In her 2019 book *Always On: Practicing Faith in a New Media Landscape*, practical theologian Angela Gorrell calls for "interested conversation" within the church about social and online media. This conversation acknowledges both the "glorious possibilities" and the "profound brokenness" present on the internet, along with the presence of God; as Gorrell puts it, "God is online."[1] Because of the human and divine presences mediated through the internet, Gorrell proposes that questions of how we engage with new media be treated seriously.

Part of interested conversation is recognizing the ways online and offline life are related and interpenetrate each other. Gorrell describes this relationship as a kind of hybridity and points out, "Most Americans live hybrid lives because our online and offline lives have become integrated. Interactions online shape offline experiences, and offline communication and practices shape people's online engagement." This hybridity is already in play in our individual lives, our families, our work, our communities, and our society. Gorrell acknowledges that humans have used various tools and media to communicate throughout history. At the same time, she suggests that there are significant differences in "new media hybrid living." Today, people use

---

[1] Angela Gorrell, *Always On: Practicing Faith in a New Media Landscape* (Grand Rapids, MI: Baker Academic, 2019), 11-12, 18.

Hybridity and Church Music

new media with very high frequency, in many different modes and expressions, and information is spread through these media extremely quickly.[2]

Similar to the discussion of virtual environments in chapter three, Gorrell contends that hybrid living has become normal for most of society, "because the Internet functions like a place." The internet possesses characteristics and performs functions of physical public and private spaces that mediate human relationships. The internet mediates these human relationships and allows for formative interactions and community building; therefore, meaningful conversation about the ongoing integration of the internet into our lives is essential.[3] This integration also takes place within Christian communities; Gorrell proposes a vision for "hybrid Christian communities" being a normative expression of faith, all the way back to Paul's letters to the "body of Christ" dispersed around the known world. This body of Christ has always been connected via a combination of in-person relationships and mediated communion, both through letters and the bread and cup. Gorrell traces the possibility and necessity of mediated community from the beginning of the church through to our current adjustments to the arrival of digital media.[4]

This kind of "hybrid faithful living," Gorrell contends, reshapes many of the church's accustomed structures. A church that espouses a dualistic view of offline versus online will have "mission statements, staff job descriptions, activities, worship services, and programs that are imagined in narrow terms (e.g., relating to in-person interactions only) and performed in physical spaces (usually within the walls of a single building)." On the other hand, communities committed to hybrid faithful living "aim to join in Jesus's ministry of holistic healing and conduct ministry in both physical and digital spaces, during in-person and mediated communication, and through how they use both old forms of media and new media."[5] Moving from a dualistic view to a hybrid view opens us up to learn and experience new approaches to ministry more broadly.

---

[2]Gorrell, *Always On*, 47.
[3]Gorrell, *Always On*, 49.
[4]Gorrell, *Always On*, 49-51.
[5]Gorrell, *Always On*, 136.

NEW EXPRESSIONS OF HYBRIDITY: CHURCH "ONLIFE" SINCE COVID-19

For the church to adapt and thrive in a world of online and digital media, there will certainly be some degree of change and learning required (though how much and what form will vary from context to context). While it is likely that the process of integrating offline and online expressions of the church would have continued to grow gradually in the coming decades, the arrival of the Covid-19 pandemic accelerated this process exponentially. Suddenly, churches were forced into online spaces that felt unfamiliar as they navigated new ways of sharing community, performing rituals, and participating in worship. Church leaders were faced with questions about online religion that were no longer hypothetical but practical. How would they meet the needs of their communities, and how would they reflect on and make meaning of the new mediated practices they were already engaged in?

Heidi A. Campbell and Wendi Bellar describe the role that online church functions took in diverse faith communities early in the pandemic. Many Christian pastors spoke of the church as "an offline community, which temporarily needed to be transformed into an online community to meet the needs of its people at that moment." While both online and offline church practices were seen as positive, they were largely perceived as "distinct and separate entities, differing vastly from one another in their character."[6] When "doing church online" was a new and strange experience for most people, it was easy to view it as very different from the offline church meetings that were so suddenly interrupted by the pandemic lockdown. The shock and change of crisis marked this new religious expression off from our accustomed practices. Given our collective traumatic experience, it makes sense that integrating these two religious expressions would be challenging and take ongoing work.

It is understandable that, for many churches and individuals, the idea of getting "back to normal" had a powerful draw. Online church felt to many like a poor substitute for the familiar format of a Sunday gathering. Campbell and Bellar note that another common point of discussion was the question of whether online worship and community were legitimate manifestations of the church people had experienced before. They report, "Many Pastors and Rabbis

---

[6] Heidi A. Campbell and Wendi Bellar, *Digital Religion: The Basics* (London: Routledge, 2022), 28.

noted that preference should be given to the offline expression as the established and preferred form of church/synagogue and online as only a stopgap or transient expression." This understanding began to give way to a new perspective on online gatherings: "By spring 2021 . . . some leaders notably changed their initial response to describe how meeting online created new forms of community interactions and investments that should not be overlooked." These new benefits included former members of worshiping communities returning to join in worship online. This allowed for people whose schedules, geographic location, or physical health prohibited them from attending in person to still engage with a community that was important to them.[7]

The combination of offline and online engagement in community is becoming a hallmark of religious expression. The internet is increasingly a part of our daily routines and "in-person" activities. Campbell and Bellar suggest, "The online-offline distinction is blurred as the Internet has become embedded in everyday realities. . . . The dualistic [view] of the online versus the offline no longer holds true for many." The offline and online aspects of our lives, and more particularly our experiences of faith and community, are connected as "an embedded online-offline reality that calls a new hybrid space into being, what Luciano Floridi . . . calls 'onlife.' Here religion can be lived and practiced between time-honored affiliations and mediated, digitally born networks of connection."[8]

MUSIC IN THE MULTIMEDIA-VERSE

Instead of persisting in binary, dichotomous thinking, churches will need to negotiate each of these spectra—around participation, embodiment, mediation, and virtuality—in their unique cultural contexts. They can do so by reflecting on, enacting, and learning through new questions, such as:

> What might it look like for our musical worship and ministry to . . .
>
> . . . invite participation in meaningful interactive and interpassive ways?
>
> . . . celebrate embodied engagement that is inclusive and holistic?
>
> . . . cultivate a positive relationship with mediation that acknowledges and respects the glorious immediacy of life in a world filled with many kinds of media, new and old?

---

[7]Campbell and Bellar, *Digital Religion*, 28-29.
[8]Campbell and Bellar, *Digital Religion*, 64-65.

. . . draw worshipers to live out the reality of their faith in a God who summons them to share the love of Christ, whether the architecture involved is built from bricks or pixels?

These questions may still seem like a bridge too far for some readers; however, in what follows I hope to offer some suggestions of helpful framings for the integration of various forms of ministry to which we are accustomed along with new forms of digital practice. The specific manifestations of this integration will depend on the context, communities, and capacities of each group of worshipers.

If church life and ministry are becoming a hybrid of online and offline interactions, this will certainly affect the church's music as well. The church is still in the beginning stages of discerning this impact, and more new expressions of musical worship will appear and develop over time. The advent of the printing press, radio, and television all influenced the church's music, opening up new possibilities and generating change. The technological revolution brought about by the internet and related technologies will lead to yet more transformations.

POTENTIAL PURPOSES OF CHURCH MUSIC

Music's multivalent nature allows it to communicate many meanings. People therefore engage with practices of church music for differing reasons and motivations. Partly based on the work of practical theologians of music such as C. Randall Bradley and Brian Wren, I have attempted to make a list that covers many (though perhaps not all) of these purposes.[9] Church music may be directed toward the purposes of

- glorifying God
- (trans)formation

---

[9] C. Randall Bradley, *From Memory to Imagination: Reforming the Church's Music* (Grand Rapids, MI: Eerdmans, 2012), 101-9. Bradley expands on two lists of characteristics of church music: "What the Music of the Church Should Do" (i.e., our music should direct us to God) and "What Music Can Do" (i.e., music has the power to create unity within a community).

Brian A. Wren, *Praying Twice: The Music and Words of Congregational Song* (Louisville, KY: Westminster John Knox, 2000), 39-66. Wren describes congregational song or church music as able to do multiple things: encourage/inspire the church and form spirituality and theology; build faith and identity; change our mental state in helpful ways; change our bodily state and enable movement; help us make meaning of life; facilitate embodied experience; dramatize and unfold the Christian story in time; express, evoke, and form our emotional lives; facilitate growth into right relationships with God and others; serve God's purposes in the church's worship, fellowship, and mission; and be corporate, corporeal, inclusive, ecclesial, inspirational, and evangelical.

- community
- closeness or relationship with God
- encouragement or edification
- theological or intellectual engagement
- emotional or affective engagement
- bodily engagement
- integrative or holistic engagement
- inclusion, accessibility, and/or participation
- excellence or beauty

In the following section I will briefly expand on what each of these terms connotes.

Glorifying God. Bringing glory to God is perhaps one of the most common purposes Christians think of when they consider church music. Our worship is meant to ascribe worth to God, to proclaim God's goodness and character, to praise God, and to thank God for the gifts of creation, redemption, and new creation. Whether this is a primary goal or a product of aiming at a different goal, this value will almost certainly appear in some form in most philosophies of church music.[10]

(Trans)formation. Formation or transformation are more human-focused values in that they consider how music shapes the character, affect, and behavior of participants. They can also involve God to the degree that the Holy Spirit is perceived to be active in this transformative work. Formation can include emotional, intellectual, or bodily implications, and it often conveys an expectation of behavioral responses to God encountered in musical worship practices. This value is fairly broad and easily overlaps or is interpreted through other values.[11]

Community. Community is likewise more human-centric, as it prioritizes the positive impacts music can have on forming, strengthening, and directing human relationships. Both Bradley and Wren discuss this value, and it also

---

[10]Constance M. Cherry, *The Music Architect: Blueprints for Engaging Worshipers in Song* (Grand Rapids, MI: Baker Academic, 2016); Bradley, *From Memory to Imagination*; Harold M. Best, *Music Through the Eyes of Faith* (San Francisco: HarperSanFrancisco, 1993).

[11]David Lemley, *Becoming What We Sing: Formation Through Contemporary Worship Music* (Grand Rapids, MI: Eerdmans, 2021); Nathan Myrick, *Music for Others: Care, Justice, and Relational Ethics in Christian Music* (London: Oxford University Press, 2021).

appears in nonreligious discussions of musicking. This category has the advantage (or disadvantage) of being malleable to religious and nonreligious contexts, and it is measured and studied through a variety of disciplines and scientific methods.[12]

Closeness or relationship with God. This is a value held very highly in some expressions of church music, but some form of this value will likely appear in most contexts. It is a goal that combines a focus on God with a human (often individual) desire to connect with God on a personal level. In some contexts, church music is the primary vehicle for experiencing God's presence, while in others it takes a more supplementary or supporting role.

Encouragement or edification. These are closely related values that speak generally to the ways that church music can equip or strengthen the people of God. In this value, music serves to enhance or support believers' living out their faith. This can take a wide variety of forms and can include either expressing the struggles of life musically or attempting to transcend or sublimate them.

Theological or intellectual engagement. Edification can also overlap with theological or intellectual engagement. This most often refers specifically to the texts associated with worship music. Those who prioritize this value will favor texts that are theologically dense, thought provoking, or didactic. In rare cases, theological or intellectual formation may involve instrumental music, perhaps placed in a liturgical context or alongside a text for consideration that directs and shapes its most likely reception by the congregation. There can also be different styles of theological/intellectual engagement; even simple and repetitive texts can express profound theological insights, and reflecting on them repeatedly may bring new perspective and integration.[13]

Emotional or affective engagement. This purpose can also fall under the broader categories of formation or relationship with God or community. These various expressions can be thought of as emotional realities that are

---

[12] Monique Marie Ingalls, *Singing the Congregation: How Contemporary Worship Music Forms Evangelical Community* (New York: Oxford University Press, 2018); Mark James Porter, *Contemporary Worship Music and Everyday Musical Lives*, Ashgate Congregational Music Studies (London: Routledge, 2017).

[13] Don Hustad, *True Worship: Reclaiming the Wonder and Majesty* (Wheaton, IL: H. Shaw, 1998); Debra Rienstra et al., *Worship Words: Discipling Language for Faithful Ministry* (Grand Rapids, MI: Baker Academic, 2009); Marva J. Dawn, *Reaching Out Without Dumbing Down: A Theology of Worship for the Turn-of-the-Century Culture* (Grand Rapids, MI: Eerdmans, 1995).

facilitated and expressed by music. Music is for many people a powerful means by which they experience and deepen their emotional life. This can also be a source of discomfort or anxiety, as some Christian traditions have developed and passed down attitudes of suspicion around human bodily responses to music and the power of emotions.

Bodily engagement. This is a particularly thorny issue for church music. There are powerful social norms around how one ought to use one's body in worship. These vary widely based on context, and what is holy in one community may be profane or insufficient in another. Music does have the potential to involve our bodies in our faith, which in contexts such as the White Western church often includes an unfortunate degree of distance from bodily realities.[14]

Integrative or holistic engagement. By this I mean the potential goal of incorporating intellectual, emotional, bodily, spiritual, and social responses in the music of the church. Broadly speaking, one can argue that worship has the potential to form worshipers to be more fully human by becoming more Christlike. This means that all our faculties are important in worship, and it may be that if we are lacking in one of these, our worship of God will become more whole by learning and growing in an area that may not come naturally to us. It also implies gaining wisdom from others who worship in ways unlike ours.

Inclusion, accessibility, and/or participation. These three are closely related values in church music. They are also contextual; what feels accessible and participatory to one individual or community will not to another. These values prioritize the ability of all people to be engaged in the church's worship and inspire ministers and leaders to lower or remove barriers to full engagement. Practically speaking, however, this value is often tempered by pragmatic considerations of what is perceived as expedient, socially normative, or economically viable.

Excellence or beauty. Excellence and beauty are often cited as values in the church's music. This is often framed theologically, as musical excellence and beauty are said to express something of God's excellence and beauty. It therefore becomes important for the church's music to measure up to

---

[14]Marcell Silva Steuernagel, *Church Music Through the Lens of Performance*, Congregational Music Studies (London: Routledge, 2021).

whichever human standard of beauty is perceived as closest to God's standard of beauty. This is both a wonderful opportunity of music, as the beauty we encounter in this varied art form can enable us to encounter something wonderful and even divine; and a perennial stumbling block, as our human shortsightedness and vanity limit our perception of what God's transcendence is truly like. At their best, excellence and beauty in the church's music become ways to reach beyond themselves for God's grandeur. At their worst, they become stifling boxes that attempt to contain God and exclude outsiders.[15]

These values should not be thought of as mutually exclusive but as at times complementary and at times conflicting, depending on their expression. I offer the metaphor of a series of lenses, some providing magnification of the object in view, others tinting the light that passes through them. These lenses are all part of the minister's/worshiper's conceptual toolbox. They can be ordered in a variety of ways, and a particular occasion or context may call for one or more of them to be used. We may favor a particular lens that we habitually reach for, but a new circumstance may move us to make use of a different configuration. Each potential permutation may draw our attention to new truths or distortions in our understanding or experience of God, our human relationships with ourselves and others, and the practical manifestations of our lived faith.

Discerning a philosophy of church music will help to guide contextual decisions about how online media can be helpfully used within the church's worship. Even once a particular church has discerned its organizing values around church music, there remains the question of how, or even whether, these values can be realized online. While there are many purposes of church music, one that is particularly salient in questions around online and hybrid musicking is the purpose of forming community.

NETWORK TEST: CRITERIA FOR EVALUATING ONLINE RITUAL PRACTICES

One of the values of religious rituals is community formation. Whether rituals are effective can be evaluated by multiple criteria; some might include

---

[15]Best, *Music Through the Eyes of Faith*; Don Hustad, *Jubilate II: Church Music in Worship and Renewal* (Carol Stream, IL: Hope, 1993); Jonathan Dueck, *Congregational Music, Conflict, and Community*, Congregational Music Studies (London: Routledge, 2017).

participation, shared emotional engagement and embodied response, and formation toward values such as caregiving, generosity, and justice. The Covid-19 pandemic has raised questions about whether and how these ritual values can be expressed or nurtured through online religious practices.

Questions about the legitimacy and effectiveness of religious practices commonly appear in times of change. In her book *Singing the Congregation*, Monique Ingalls engages with a seismic cultural and technological shift that transformed the landscape of Christian worship music: the growth of the contemporary worship music industry. She references a magazine article written by Marshall Shelly that raised questions about how worship could be determined to be authentic. Ingalls discusses how these criteria—"that worship must be God centered, participatory, and personally transformative"—can provide metrics for whether a concert could be properly understood as worship.[16]

This set of criteria can be usefully adapted to apply to online worship practices and music. They originally were aimed at determining whether a worship gathering or concert was authentic worship in light of musical worship being mediated through new cultural and technological forms. Now they may serve us in discerning whether and how online media can be used with integrity toward Christian formation.

Randall Bradley has an additional insight to offer regarding communal worship. In his book *From Memory to Imagination: Reforming the Church's Music*, Bradley reflects on the importance of genuine community in the midst of an individualistic culture and music industry: "Sometimes communal worship is mistaken for individual worship that happens to take place in the company of others. Communal worship implies that there is mutual exchange, mutual dependence, and a synergy that results in 'the sum being greater than its parts.'"[17] Bradley's argument is that mere proximity of physical presence does not make worship communal. Given that, one could also argue the converse: that physical distance may not necessarily preclude the possibility of a communal practice. Mutual exchange and dependence,

---

[16] Ingalls, *Singing the Congregation*, 48. Ingalls goes on to discuss how such criteria are complicated by the worship industry's use of them to authenticate their products as genuine worship experiences. Even though these criteria can be problematized, they still provide a valuable starting point.

[17] Bradley, *From Memory to Imagination*, 170.

and a synergistic whole greater than the sum of its parts, can occur through online mediated means. As discussed in previous chapters, embodiment is not negated by mediation. The same can be said about embodiment regarding communal proximity and mediation: proximity does not guarantee a high degree of embodied engagement or mindful presence, and distance does not rule out the potential for embodiment.

In *The Distanced Church: Reflections on Doing Church Online*, Arni Svanur Danielsson writes about the importance of connection and savvy use of available communication technology. Regardless of whether communication is face to face or online, Danielsson argues that several principles hold true: "You need to 1) know your audience, 2) know your medium or 'know your space,' 3) know your message, and 4) engage and empower your audience to, 5) nurture a connection." He suggests that worship leaders are already well equipped to understand their audiences and messages but less confident in using the medium or space of online interactions. Danielsson invites church leaders to "take a page out of the playbooks of YouTubers, gamers who livestream, or influencers on platforms like Instagram."[18]

Bringing these insights together, the following diagnostic questions can serve as valuable criteria for evaluating online religious practices. First, is this practice genuinely participatory? In other words, does it facilitate engagement, whether in interactive or interpassive senses, or some combination of the two? Second, is this practice personally transformative? Do participants experience this practice as something that has bearing on their behavior and their lives? Third, does this practice effectively use the relevant medium for communication and connection? Does it take advantage of the affordances of that medium and avoid or minimize its weaknesses? Fourth, is this online practice God centered? This criterion will be influenced by the theology of the given community; it also will not apply in cases of nonreligious communities, such as some of the examples I will provide in the next chapter.

The question of what makes worship corporate is not just whether a practice is done in the presence of other people but whether a practice shapes participants into a relational posture. I argue that the measure of a communal

---

[18] Arni Svanur Danielsson, "Connection Trumps Technology," in *The Distanced Church: Reflections on Doing Church Online*, ed. Heidi Campbell (n.p.: Digital Religion, 2020), 10, https://doi.org/10.21423/distancedchurch.

Hybridity and Church Music 121

practice is not in the quantity of people within a particular square footage but the quality of relationships nurtured and expressed through that practice. If Heidi Campbell is correct, these relationships of religious community in the current media landscape can be best understood as a network of connections. One measure of the effectiveness or health of a communal practice, then, is the fruit produced by that networked community in building relationships and seeking justice and flourishing life. To restate my criteria in a condensed way, effective online communal practices are

1. participatory (i.e., prompting physiological responses, emotional expression, and dialogue);
2. transformative (individuals or groups expressing changed values, beliefs, or desires following the digital experience, or acting in ways that demonstrate this change);
3. appropriate to the medium (utilizing the strengths/main practices of the medium; its affordances); and perhaps
4. centered on God (invites theological reflection and/or engagement in spiritual disciplines or practices) or another shared value (is intentionally organized around particular value[s]).[19]

Effective worship leaders already aspire to these values in their musical ministries. They hope that people in their communities will feel empowered, invited, and inspired to participate in a variety of ways, whether singing with congregational music on Sunday mornings, volunteering to play instruments and sing in choirs and ensembles, or joining in with musical opportunities to connect with communities and causes in their broader contexts. They want to model and cultivate a rich spiritual and emotional life in the congregations they lead, and music is a key tool for expressing and nurturing that depth of meaning, connection, and conversation. These faithful leaders hope their communities will encounter God in transformative ways, and they craft worship experiences directed toward that goal. They also do what they can to lead in ways that are appropriate in their context. This includes the individuals in their communities, the musical resources available to them, and the values and other ministries of their churches. For most of us, this

---

[19] These criteria were developed in a directed study with Rev. Dr. Angela Gorrell in May 2023.

contextual awareness is the area with the most room for growth in the twenty-first century.

A piece of good news is that there are individuals and communities that are excelling in online contexts and can be helpful models for us. As Danielsson suggests, we can learn from these streamers, podcasters, and artists how to better engage with others online. In the following chapter, I will describe online communities that exhibit effective community formation. These communities have varied levels of involvement with religion, from completely secular, to adjacent to major religious traditions, to operating within typical church contexts. These case studies will examine how each community utilizes the affordances of various media platforms in effective ways to build meaningful relationships through online interactions while using music. Exploring these examples will lead into reflection on the ways Christian music ministry can more effectively make use of the affordances of online media.

Online Ritual Communities

IN EARLY 2020, AS our lives changed in response to the threat of Covid-19, my Sunday school class, largely made up of twenty- and thirty-something graduate students and young parents, had to find new ways to connect while we were physically apart. Looking back on this period now, I find it somewhat strange to realize that the time I spent interacting with this small community, and my church community more broadly, did not disappear when the pandemic appeared. Instead, it shifted. Rather than an hour spent together from nine to ten a.m. each Sunday morning, our relationships bled into other minutes of our daily lives. Ongoing texts, check-ins to see how we each were doing, FaceTime calls, and group video messages through an app called Marco Polo established an ongoing relational tether. We were encouraged and sustained by this community, whether we were sharing prayer requests and updates about our families or laughing at one of our member's parody cooking videos (I don't recommend washing raw chicken with Dawn soap before cooking it, but it made for a memorable story! Thanks, Ethan).

We were experiencing the hybridity of our relationships, tilted in an extraordinary way toward the online while our habitual offline contact was paused for a time. And while this time was fraught with tension, fears, and the exhaustion brought on by collective upheaval and trauma, it was also a precious expression of our little community. When I share a coffee with some of these people now in 2024, it is not uncommon for our conversation to touch on those strange days, when we shared a special connection despite our physical separation.

As noted in chapter four, one of the important values expressed in church music is building community. When asked about the complexities of online worship practices, Heidi Campbell recognized the importance of this value and the way its presence or absence became critical during early expressions of online church:

> "What is community?" is . . . one of the big questions. Because a lot of people found . . . we're using social media, but we haven't actually created a social experience . . . and [were] realizing the technology itself, just because you use it doesn't mean it's going to create that. You actually have to design it in or culture that in. And so a lot of people began to talk about [how] before the pandemic, the community [was] the gathered people, and the gathered people being a physical kind of gathering, and then people later in the pandemic [began] saying, gathering can happen in different forms and saying, okay, what is it about the offline presence that we value, and how can we replicate that? But there's a real rethinking of what it means to gather.[1]

As Campbell highlights, this conversation around the sense of community created through—or lacking in—online rituals has continued to develop in recent years. The American church overall is new at this; we are not experts when it comes to fostering community in digital interactions. There remains much more experimentation and reflection to be done.

One way we can continue this learning process is by attending to and being curious about expressions of online community outside the church. Online communities outside the church highlight how networks of connections can function to build community through rituals. The following three case studies show that genuine community formation can happen through digital media. The first is from a video game livestream on the platform Twitch.tv, the primary website for viewing live gameplay footage. The second relates to a podcast community that combines online and offline interactions. The third grows out of a singer-songwriter's Patreon page, on which fans can support the artist's work and gain access to patron-only updates, messages, and vlogs. Each of these online communal practices makes excellent use of the affordances and unique strengths of its media platform to connect people to one another. These three examples differ in scale, as well as in the practices

---

[1] Heidi A. Campbell, interview by author, Zoom, January 20, 2023.

they engage with to form community. Each may provide useful insights as religious communities attempt to build connection both online and offline. Together, these ethnographies can help us see how to faithfully build community in light of the hybrid world we inhabit.

"CLOSE IN THE DISTANCE": DIGITAL PRESENCE AND COMMUNAL AFFECT ON TWITCH.TV

In church music studies, questions of music's role in community building, ritual participation, and collaboration are familiar and significant, and in recent years, concerns about how these functions of music can occur through online media have become live and pressing questions.[2] It now seems important to examine these dynamics more closely. As we consider how music can be used via online media to facilitate community and identity formation in religious contexts, we can also ask how music and online media are being used in nonreligious communities and what has proven effective. Some particular questions that are important around digitally mediated music include: Can digitally mediated music induce embodied responses, genuine participation, and communal affect? Can it be a factor in the formation of shared communal values, identities, and narratives leading to social action?

The first case study will explore a video game stream hosted on the website Twitch.tv, which offers promising examples of collaboration, participation, and community formation through digitally mediated video game music. I will then explore the broader network of online interactions taking place around this community and examine how this community has real-world impact.

This case study centers on a Twitch video game streamer who goes by the username ZeplaHQ, and the communal chat responses to her live gameplay of the massively multiplayer online roleplaying game *Final Fantasy XIV*. This live chat and surrounding asynchronous communication reveals a

---

[2] Anna E. Nekola and Thomas Wagner, eds., *Congregational Music-Making and Community in a Mediated Age*, Ashgate Congregational Music Studies (Farnham, UK: Routledge, 2015); Monique Marie Ingalls, *Singing the Congregation: How Contemporary Worship Music Forms Evangelical Community* (New York: Oxford University Press, 2018); Heidi A. Campbell and John Dyer, eds., *Ecclesiology for a Digital Church* (London: SCM Press, 2021); Heidi A. Campbell, *Digital Religion: Understanding Religious Practice in New Media Worlds* (New York: Routledge, 2013).

communal ecosystem that responds to music with shared embodied and affective responses, emotional support, and tangible expressions of generosity and hospitality in response to real-world crises.

Final Fantasy XIV is a fantasy video game developed by Square Enix and appreciated by its fanbase for its compelling storytelling and character development. In contrast to many online games that focus on competitive multiplayer gameplay or optimizing a character's abilities to maximize their combat effectiveness, *Final Fantasy XIV* places a heavy emphasis on the narrative, experienced similarly by every player. All players take the role of the hero in the story and journey through the same narrative beats with the same cast of fictional characters. This leads to solidarity between players, who experience communal engagement with the story as a point of connection. There are powerful social norms within the game's community that heavily dissuade anyone from spoiling the story for another player or pressuring them to speed through the game's narrative content. *Final Fantasy XIV*'s community relishes the shared narrative, though large portions of the story are experienced individually.

The game's *Endwalker* expansion (analogous to a new season of a Netflix show) released in November 2021 to overwhelmingly positive critical and fan response. The plot is the culmination of a ten-year-long story arc, drawing together threads from the past decade and carrying significant emotional weight. The climax of this story features the song "Close in the Distance" by composer Masayoshi Soken, who scored the music for the expansion. The stream I viewed for this research featured ZeplaHQ, a female gamer living in Ukraine, playing through the narrative climax of the *Endwalker* expansion.

The typical Twitch streaming format includes video and audio of the streamer who is playing the game, a screen recording of their computer monitor, and a text chat including emojis and typed messages from viewers. Twitch streams are typically interactive, with the streamer reading and responding to the chat throughout their gameplay. The original live video from the Twitch platform was recorded and uploaded to YouTube on December 28, 2021. As of this writing, the five-and-a-half-hour YouTube video has 420,000 views and more than a thousand comments.[3]

---

[3]ZepLIVE, "Zepla Playthrough of Endwalker MSQ—The Final Day (Timestamps Inside)," December 28, 2021, video, 5:38:11, www.youtube.com/watch?v=JhzyzPCRwng.

After playing through the *Endwalker* story myself, I suspected that a particular moment in the story would have elicited significant engagement from stream viewers. This moment features a beloved character from the *Final Fantasy XIV* story sacrificing himself to ensure the player will be able to achieve victory in saving the universe. The story beat is underscored with emotionally charged music that draws on the musical motifs and narrative themes developed through the game's decade-long story.

Thematically, the *Endwalker* expansion closely mirrors common experiences of the Covid-19 pandemic, as the heroes battle with a deadly plague and the looming threats of hopelessness, isolation, and existential despair. This moment also deals with questions of our continued humanity in the face of personal change, loss, and technological advances. As the character gives his final speech, the Twitch viewers in the chat reflect on their emotional responses to this moment in their own gameplay experience and discuss the overall impact of the *Endwalker* expansion in light of tragic world events. The streamer, Zepla, is visibly moved as the scene progresses, and participants in the chat both share their own emotional responses and react to hers.

I want to highlight several patterns in these live chat responses as they relate to music, community, participation, and processing and sharing life experiences. More of these chat responses can be found in the appendix.

First, these responses demonstrate powerful anticipation of the music about to play in this scene. Twitch viewers made chat comments such as "the music is coming," "It's time for the music," and "HERE WE GO." Second, they express strong identification with and ownership of this music as personally significant, saying "OUR SONG," "I have this song on repeat all the time," and "help I've been listening to this song on repeat for days." Third, these responses are unequivocally embodied, even though digitally mediated. Viewers shared messages such as "Here comes the flood of tears [crying emoji]," "somebody hold me," "I'll hold you," and "You're crying, I'm crying, everybody is crying."[4]

These Twitch viewers are not exaggerating when they report that they are crying—having experienced the same story, I found myself in tears again just

---

[4] ZepLIVE, "Zepla Playthrough of Endwalker MSQ."

reading the transcription of the chat, much less watching the story play out. In his book *The Power of Ritual: Turning Everyday Activities into Soulful Practices*, Casper ter Kuile writes, "Nothing is more indicative of a community taking shape than when people feel free to cry in front of others. . . . Our bodies are doing the speaking. In a culture that values rationality and dismisses emotion as untrustworthy, it has become difficult to access our vulnerable core through words and thoughts alone, and especially in public."[5] One might argue that these Twitch viewers are not crying in front of others but rather are crying alone. However, if that were how they experienced this moment, it would have been quite easy for all of them to remain silent in the chat and keep their tears private.

Instead, a huge number of them actively chose to express their emotional, embodied, physiological response with an online community of people gathered around this shared story and music. They chose to share their emotions through text, making both requests and offers for physical support ("somebody hold me," "I'll hold you," "let's hold hands chat," "ahwww zepla big hug"). Obviously, this was not literal physical support, but it was offered and received as genuine emotional support.

They also expressed themselves through emojis (crying face emojis, heart emojis, and the "catjam" emoji) that serve as shorthand for articulating bodily attitudes and expressions. When these Twitch viewers used what I transcribed as [catjam emoji], they were sharing a small .gif of a meme, originally from Instagram. It depicts a cat bobbing its head in a rhythmic manner, as if listening to music with a pronounced beat. The primary reason it would even occur to an internet user to remember and reference the meme is that they felt a similar rhythmic entrainment in their own body. This meme is internet shorthand for active physical engagement with music, particularly with a driving rhythm or groove, and often with positive or powerful affect. It mimics and expresses the communal entrainment a crowd of concertgoers experiences when jamming or vibing along to a live, in-person performance. This embodied muscle memory associated with musical affect is an example of the body schema concept discussed in chapter two. This meme is a part of some digital natives' body schemas, including my own. Not all internet users

---

[5] Casper ter Kuile, *The Power of Ritual: Turning Everyday Activities into Soulful Practices* (New York: HarperOne, 2020), 100.

will connect with the same memes and cultural references, but sharing in these common experiences is one of the ways community is simultaneously mediated and embodied online.

This use of emojis in combination with written messages represents a development in the technology of writing on the internet. Steve Taylor argues that this reintroduces a greater degree of embodied engagement into writing:

> The presence of Internet acronyms, chat, emojis and GIFs (Graphics Interchange Format) changes the way we communicate . . . writing is a technology. As technologies evolve, writing will change. "Once we had the technology to send any image anywhere, we used it to restore our bodies to our writing, to give a sense of who's talking and what mood we're in when we're saying things." . . . Hence the digital shift generates a search for more holistic and enfleshed forms of communication. Written language is now more embodied, relational and emotionally laden. Fuller expressions of being human are possible.[6]

It is intriguing to note that digital written communication has great potential for expressing and communicating embodiment. It may be different from handwritten communication (such as Paul's statement in Galatians 6:11, "See what large letters I make when I am writing in my own hand!"), but we can learn to utilize it more effectively in our efforts to build community and love others well. These Twitch stream viewers found embodied ways to show up for each other.

Fourth, these viewers were actively engaged with the music through the means at their disposal. They expressed through text how they were participating in the music that was affecting them emotionally. The others watching the stream could not hear them singing along, but they circumvented this obstacle by typing lyrics of the song in the chat, sometimes with additional letters to signal the sustained vocalization of singing, that is, "tails [sic] of loooooss and fiiiiire and faaaith [catjam emoji]."[7]

Fifth, it is interesting to note that multiple viewers referenced a sense that they were "doing this again," implying that watching someone else play the game was as emotionally affecting and engaging as playing it themselves. This speaks to the interpassive element of viewing online streaming content.

---

[6]Steve Taylor, "Lockdown Ecclesiologies: The Limits and Possibilities of Enforced Online First Expressions," in Campbell and Dyer, *Ecclesiology for a Digital Church*, 163.
[7]ZepLIVE, "Zepla Playthrough of Endwalker MSQ."

The phenomenon of "Let's Play" streams and videos has recently been examined through the concept of interpassivity. I will briefly refresh that discussion here. Robert Pfaller has been a major proponent of interpassivity as a useful framework; at the opening of his 2017 book *Interpassivity: The Aesthetics of Delegated Enjoyment*, he describes how delegating *work* to others is a common feature of our society. Pfaller goes on to attempt an explanation for confusing dynamics that seem to involve, rather than a delegation of *work*, a delegation of *consumption* or *enjoyment*. Pfaller describes this as "a pleasant consuming attitude . . . a 'passivity.' . . . The *enjoyment* of something is—partly or even totally—delegated to other people or to a technical device."[8]

Alex Gekker draws on this idea of interpassivity specifically in reference to video game streams. In "Let's Not Play: Interpassivity as Resistance in 'Let's Play' Videos," Gekker examines streams and videos of recorded gameplay: "[Viewing a Let's Play video] 'triggers what one could call ludic immersion through non-ludic engagement.' . . . In other words, the LPer [Let's Player] acts, if not as proxy, then at least as an emotional compass for the spectator."[9] This dynamic of interpassive immersion is central to how video game streams work; rather than playing a game themselves, stream viewers delegate the enjoyment of play to someone else. The interpassive element informs how collaboration and participation function in this particular digital context. A Twitch stream can in theory become a locus for the formation of a networked community, unbounded by spatial limits, through combined interactive and interpassive participation. The interpassive connection between the Twitch streamer Zepla and the viewers engaging in the chat was an essential factor in this community forming.

Sixth, the Twitch viewers connected their experience of this music with the composer's life experiences, reinforcing the communal narrative and values they were creating. Along with the streamer Zepla, the composer became another model and emotional compass as the broader community around the game used his music to process and share their own struggles.

---

[8] Robert Pfaller, *Interpassivity: The Aesthetics of Delegated Enjoyment* (Edinburgh: Edinburgh University Press, 2017), chapter 1, Kindle.
[9] Alex Gekker, "Let's Not Play: Interpassivity as Resistance in 'Let's Play' Videos," *Journal of Gaming & Virtual Worlds* 10, no. 3 (2018): 231.

The Twitch viewers and other online community members referenced the composer Soken's battle with cancer, using the hashtag #WelcomeBackSoken. This hashtag refers to his time in the hospital, during which he composed at least some of the music for the *Endwalker* expansion. A YouTube user named Kong Chang commented on another *Final Fantasy XIV*–related YouTube video, "I still can't believe Soken composed his best work from the hospital. . . . #WelcomeBackSoken." Other YouTube comments fill out the picture of this song's community reception, saying things such as, "nothing sounds more like 'growing hope' than this!" and "Almost cried my eyes out playing through this. . . . It's been a whole month since I finished [*Endwalker*], still can't listen to this song without tearing up." Other viewer comments highlighted the roles the *Endwalker* story, and this song in particular, played in significant life events and struggles.[10]

These Twitch and YouTube viewers shared a powerful, affective, embodied experience through these videos and online interactions. They offered and received emotional support, and used this music and story, as well as the composer's experience and artistry, as resources to make meaning in their own lives. This online community felt the limitations of the digital medium coming between their shared emotional expression and found ways to overcome those limitations to share meaningful connection over an experience that mattered to them. Though they were far apart, they experienced a moment of communal engagement and were "close in the distance."

Significantly, the communal engagement extends offline, as members provide physical, emotional, and monetary assistance to other members of their community. Two months later Russia invaded Ukraine, where the streamer Zepla had lived for eight years (specifically in Kyiv). On February 24, 2022, Zepla posted on her Twitter account, "I hear air raid sirens !! Terrifying sound i hoped to never hear in my life. But we are in the car leaving now!!!! I only pray the polish border authority lets us pass."[11] After making it to Poland, she later relocated to Portugal, where she shared an update with her YouTube viewers on March 18, 2022. In this video, she reported that she

---

[10]Work to Game, "FFXIV FanFest 2021 Was Legendary | Welcome Back Soken," May 17, 2021, video, 20:04, www.youtube.com/watch?v=RZ8l37z96qw.
[11]Mike Williams, "FFXIV Streamer Zepla Finds Refuge from Ukrainian Crisis in Poland," Fanbyte, February 24, 2022, www.fanbyte.com/news/ffxiv-streamer-zepla-hq-ukraine-safety-poland/.

cannot go back to her home in Kyiv, that her house was almost certainly looted and possibly destroyed. She described how she was unable to access her Ukrainian bank account and expressed appreciation for her viewers who were supporting her through donations and viewing ads on her Twitch channel and Patreon. Zepla described how meaningful it was to have the support of her online community as she was fleeing from her home:

> Honestly, even just offering your emotional support, and your kindness, and your kind words. . . . I've had so many of you reach out to me and, um, offer me . . . a place to stay in your house. . . . Some of you have offered your own homes to me. . . . You've offered up rooms in your own houses to me. And, uh, I honestly get kind of emotional thinking about that, because, it really . . . when I heard a lot of those messages from y'all . . . Oh, my God, I'm sorry [visibly emotional] . . . that's when I really started to feel like this is a family that we have here, like this community really is a family. And I can't thank you enough for that, that kindness, uh . . . I never felt alone. Throughout this, I have not felt alone, and I've not felt like I was without friends, I've not felt like I was without a safety net, and that's because of you. So, thank you so, so much for that. It really matters to me.[12]

Zepla also posted a list of Ukrainian charities on social media that her followers could donate to and planned charity event livestreams to support Ukrainian organizations.

This online community centered on affinity for video gaming is characterized by shared emotional investment and physiological responses, empathy and expressions of emotional and implied physical support, coming together around shared narrative and musical material to make sense of life experiences, receiving the stories of others, reducing feelings of loneliness and isolation in the face of personal loss and real-world crises, and encouraging generosity and hospitality. In his book *Becoming What We Sing: Formation Through Contemporary Worship Music*, David Lemley writes, "Worshipers have encountered an alternate reality that bears on their everyday decisions and actions."[13] This online community gathered around a video

---

[12]Zepla HQ, "I've Left Ukraine—a Personal Update," March 18, 2022, video, 15:43, www.youtube.com/watch?v=ilwDDRYBI0g.

[13]David Lemley, *Becoming What We Sing: Formation Through Contemporary Worship Music* (Grand Rapids, MI: Eerdmans, 2021), 177.

game streaming channel seems to have similarly encountered an alternate reality that inspires them to connect with each other through music and form a relational network, even to the point of offering hospitality and support to war refugees.

"A LISTENING COMMUNITY": *HARRY POTTER AND THE SACRED TEXT*

A second example of online community forming across distance can be seen around the podcast *Harry Potter and the Sacred Text*. At the beginning of 2016, a pair of Harvard Divinity School students, Vanessa Zoltan and Casper ter Kuile, organized a group that began meeting regularly for an unusual ritual: applying sacred reading techniques to a popular children's novel. Ter Kuile describes the early days of this group: "We promised one another we'd sit and read the books chapter by chapter, asking them what they might teach us about how to live. We'd use spiritual practices from antiquity . . . to dig underneath the plot to find unexpected wisdom in the wizarding world."[14]

This began as a local, in-person group of a few dozen people but soon grew into something else. Ter Kuile describes it as "a mini congregation where people made friends, visited one another in the hospital, and fell in love." After the initial success of this local group, they launched the *Harry Potter and the Sacred Text* podcast in May 2016. The show consists of a weekly conversation about a chapter of the Harry Potter books through a chosen theme, such as commitment, forgiveness, trauma, delight, or love. The hosts share a personal story related to the weekly theme, summarize the chapter, and engage the text through spiritual practices, most often from Christian or Jewish traditions.[15]

The original practice of reading together with a group in proximity expanded into an online space, which exponentially increased its reach and impact. The podcast has now reached its thirteenth season, with over four hundred episodes and seventy thousand regular weekly listeners. It also grew to include yearly tours, with live episodes of the show being recorded with in-person audiences. Ter Kuile describes the response of these listeners they

---
[14] Ter Kuile, *Power of Ritual*, 42.
[15] Ter Kuile, *Power of Ritual*, 43-44.

meet on the road, many of whom find comfort in the podcast and the familiar books in challenging times. Some engage in sacred reading practices as they process death or loss; others use these practices in their classrooms. In ter Kuile's words, "Over and over again we learn that these practices help people connect with what matters to them."[16]

In 2018, ter Kuile's cohost and cofounder of the podcast, Vanessa Zoltan, gave a presentation at the Yale Youth Ministry Institute with her professor and mentor, Stephanie Paulsell. Paulsell presented on the importance of imagination and creativity in youth ministry, describing the impact of the *Harry Potter and the Sacred Text* podcast, tours, and local reading groups. She exhorted the people present at the ministry event to "take what is new and urgent in your young people's lives and use the wisdom of ancient practices to help them take what they already love and go deeper together in community." Paulsell suggests that these young people are "already engaged in spiritual practices of imagination and creativity," and have been told that their passions are lacking meaning and significance, that they are consumers, not creators. But Paulsell argues that when young people engage with media they love repeatedly, they "are not just consuming. They are thinking, they are wondering, and through their love and devotion to these films and songs and books and videos they are engaged in a spiritual practice." She summons teachers and ministers to "help our young people recognize and have confidence in the spiritual practices that they are already doing."[17]

Harry Potter and the Sacred Text has helped numerous young people (and listeners of all ages) to engage with spiritual practices and find space for meaning-making in their lives. Paulsell also highlights the unique role that Zoltan and ter Kuile found themselves in as they interacted with this network of podcast listeners. They were surprised how engaged their audience was. These podcast hosts found themselves receiving numerous emails and voicemails from people who listened to their show. These express thanks for a show they enjoy, disagreement or feedback about a recent discussion about a chapter of *Harry Potter*, or listeners' own interpretations. Paulsell points out the deeply personal elements to some of these connections:

---

[16]Ter Kuile, *Power of Ritual*, 44.
[17]Yale Youth Ministry Institute, "Dr. Stephanie Paulsell and Vanessa Zoltan on Imagination & Creativity," June 27, 2018, video, 1:16:41, www.youtube.com/watch?v=0I755tJlakc.

Online Ritual Communities

Sometimes they tell Vanessa and Casper very difficult truths about their lives: "I was abused as a child," some write, "and reading about Harry Potter navigating his own childhood abuse helped me survive." "I was abused as a child," some write, "and it hurts me when you talk about forgiveness." "I was abused as a child, and so the *Harry Potter* books were sacred to me long before I found your podcast." Responding pastorally to this far-flung community has been one of the unexpected challenges of Vanessa's work.[18]

After the lecture, Zoltan led the attendees through a sacred reading practice of lectio divina focused on the opening line of the first *Harry Potter* book. Zoltan and Paulsell then gave a series of short interviews, responding to questions about the podcast. In a video interview on ritual and Millennials, Zoltan expresses her conviction that "people are yearning for meaning-making . . . and I really think that churches not just *can* but *need* to meet people where they are in these things."[19] In another 2018 interview on building community, Zoltan notes that she considers this ecosystem to be a network but not a community, "because you don't meet other people when you're listening to a podcast by yourself." She highlights that their goal is to bridge that gap: "We are very intentionally trying to move it from people feeling connected to each other in a virtual world to actually being in relationship with each other."[20]

Different from Heidi Campbell's description of communities in the digital age functioning primarily as networks, Zoltan uses these two terms to contrast online relationships with in-person interactions. However, the two are connected and feed into each other, and over time they have perhaps become even more closely linked.

Over the years, *Harry Potter and the Sacred Text* has continued to grow, and its creators' perspective on its role has shifted, partly in response to the Covid-19 pandemic. In a podcast conversation with Jen Hatmaker, Casper ter Kuile reflected on the community's development:

> What we found was that through media you can actually build not a congregation but certainly a listening community. We had people create local groups.

---

[18] Yale Youth Ministry Institute, "Dr. Stephanie Paulsell and Vanessa Zoltan on Imagination & Creativity."
[19] Yale Youth Ministry Institute, "Dr. Stephanie Paulsell and Ms. Vanessa Zoltan on Ritual and Millennials," July 10, 2018, video, 2:56, www.youtube.com/watch?v=q2TFIb9n6k4.
[20] Yale Youth Ministry Institute, "Dr. Stephanie Paulsell and Vanessa Zoltan on Building Community," July 10, 2018, video, 4:25, www.youtube.com/watch?v=Z4uirQkGot0.

When Covid hit, those local groups created a mutual aid fund, and people were sending, you know, real, hard cash to support other people who'd lost their job in the listening community. We raised money for good causes. Moreover, we'd get involved in political activities or justice issues, so there's ways in which you can see some of the things you would expect to see in a congregation happen in a media community.[21]

Similar to the community that formed around Zepla's gaming livestream on Twitch, this listening community gathered around *Harry Potter and the Sacred Text* fulfills multiple roles often associated with religious groups. When asked what he sees as the church's prospects, ter Kuile expresses both concern and hope for the future of organized religion:

The thing I really have hope for is the mix of kind of networks that are facilitated by digital tools and then small groups of people meeting locally. I am, like, the world's biggest fan of small groups. I think that's where transformation happens. . . . I think that's what we're gonna move towards, is maybe fewer local congregations of three hundred people, but a lot more large networks with lots and lots and lots of small groups that happen and are facilitated by that. . . . I think we're gonna see a mixed spiritual ecology, where we have some traditional institutions, lots of new things, lots of networks, hopefully lots of small groups.[22]

The image of large, networked communities—similar to Campbell's vision of relationships in the digital age—connecting numerous local small groups is a compelling one. In the case of *Harry Potter and the Sacred Text*, this model is apparently effective in connecting people to meaningful spiritual practices and to each other.

As a faithful listener of *Harry Potter and the Sacred Text*, I want to mention one other aspect of the podcast as online community that seems worthy of attention. Since the start of the Covid-19 pandemic, the podcast has introduced a section of every episode in which the hosts (ter Kuile has since moved on from the podcast, and Zoltan is now joined each week by Matthew Potts, an Episcopal priest and professor at Harvard) recite the names of listeners' loved ones who have died. Early on, this was specifically to honor

---

[21] Jen Hatmaker, "Is the Church Dead? A Millennial's Perspective on Religion with Casper ter Kuile," in *For the Love*, April 12, 2022, podcast, 1:05:20, www.youtube.com/watch?v=WEPyYdjqs70.
[22] Hatmaker, "Is the Church Dead?"

those who died due to Covid, but it has since been expanded to include personal loss due to any cause and has even occasionally included pets. Zoltan or Potts reads the names of the departed, along with a brief description submitted by their loved one, and then offers a benediction, such as, "Let light perpetual shine upon them," or "May their memories be a blessing." Each of the spiritual practices applied during the podcast, whether a form of close reading, offering blessings to characters, or taking time for remembrance of people who have passed, is framed by familiar music that reappears in each episode.

Harry Potter and the Sacred Text undergirds and connects an online community characterized by close reading of shared narrative material, seeking wisdom and applicability for daily life. Members of the larger network submit the names of their loved ones for remembrance and share voicemails that offer reflections on textual themes or blessings for characters and other community members. This network also facilitates engaging with local communities, advocating for justice, and consistently acknowledging personal and communal grief. It cultivates an attitude of reflective openness to life experiences and an expectation to encounter sacred insight in all kinds of places.

"TO SAY THAT WE'RE HERE": SPENCER LAJOYE'S PATREON

The third online community I want to describe functions on a very different scale from the previous two. Patreon is a website that allows artists and creators to request support from people who engage with their content, most often in the form of monthly subscriptions through the platform. People who subscribe to support an artist on Patreon are called patrons. These patrons typically gain access to exclusive content as a reward for their support; a $5-per-month subscription might unlock extra blog posts, or a $20-per-month subscription might earn the patron a regular conversation with the artist about their work.

One creator I support on Patreon is Spencer LaJoye, a songwriter whose tagline states that Spencer is "creating music and gentleness." On Spencer's "About" page, they write that, by becoming a patron, "you join a family of folks who believe in **revolutionary empathy**. See, I believe that **music can change the world** simply by making us feel something, and that feeling something is an act of defiance against a system that would have us go defensively numb."

Their Patreon site includes weekly blog posts, early releases of music videos, unfinished versions of songs in process, and short vlogs called "take tens." A "take ten" is a video, roughly ten minutes in length, in which Spencer shares some of their thoughts on a topic. These videos address themes such as rest, the creative process, friendship, religious trauma, boundaries, faith, and expressing challenging or complex emotions. Each "take ten" begins with a minute of silence, in which Spencer sits quietly in front of their camera, before discussing the topic for the day. Spencer provides an explanation for this silence each time; in one video, they state that its purpose is "to say that we're here and not everywhere else."[23]

The invitation to silence and stillness (though Spencer typically provides the caveat that silence may be relative for each viewer depending on their context and home situation) shapes the experience of reflection that follows. The moment is surprisingly intimate and serves as a reminder to me as a viewer to be attentive to my own body, my breathing, and my physical sensations. Though Spencer and their patrons are separated by a computer screen, this online, asynchronous practice puts me in touch with my embodied experience. Patrons can also comment on Spencer's posts and updates, sharing encouragement, responses to their reflections, and feedback on Spencer's music.

Another take ten video, posted on May 26, 2022, came the week after a mass shooting at an elementary school in Uvalde, Texas, shortly before Spencer was scheduled to perform less than one hundred miles away from Uvalde. Spencer began with their typical minute of silence and then shared some thoughts on the challenge of singing lyrics from their song "Plowshare Prayer" such as, "Amen for the kids who grow up scared of guns," and "Amen for the parents who just lost their baby," so close to this kind of tragedy:

> I'm not sure what to say. . . . Another reason is 'cause I think in these moments, as a musician . . . I feel . . . These are the moments when I should feel like my music is the most powerful . . . but for some reason these are always the moments when I'm like . . . I feel powerless. And I feel like . . . feeling something isn't enough, like making people feel something isn't enough. Which is true and false, right? Of course it's false. It means something, to feel something . . .

---

[23] Spencer LaJoye, "Spencer LaJoye Is Creating Music and Sacred Space," Patreon, accessed May 7, 2022, www.patreon.com/spencerlajoye.

to be moved to act. You have to be moved before you act. And . . . it's true because, you know . . . I struggle a little bit with the fact that I'm gonna be singing, like, a prayer song. And the whole thing right now is, "Thoughts and prayers are not enough," right? . . . I don't think it's enough for me to just offer this public prayer.[24]

Spencer then ended their video with a song titled "How Long," drawing on both psalmic texts and the prayer *Kyrie eleison; Christe eleison* ("Lord, have mercy; Christ, have mercy").

A patron then commented on Spencer's post, offering the following input:

Spencer, my first piece of advice is not to put too much pressure on yourself to come up with the "right thing" to say. You are thoughtful and empathetic and caring enough that I trust that you will find the right words in the moment. My other thought revolves around the idea you expressed about art combating apathy and how feeling something is a precursor to action. I think there is a tendency for a lot of us after news like the news about the shooting to go numb because the pain feels too great and we feel too powerless. I think music, your music, can resonate deeply with people and cause them to feel and draw them out of the numbness. And I think that there is more to your performance of Plowshare Prayer than just offering words of "thoughts and prayers." I think the song transcends that in ways I can't really explain. So maybe what you offer through your music is a moment in time where people may collectively experience some shared emotion that, perhaps, may spur some to consider what actions they might take.[25]

Another patron responded further:

Yes, Love, the choir needs support. The activists need support. The ministers and therapists and poets need support. In some ways our job is to feel, and when there is this much to feel it gets piled up and log jammed and it's like having too many programs running on my poor computer—overwhelm. Shutdown. Your music is SUCH deep support for those who feel because it helps us MOVE the feelings through—through into action. Through so that we're ready for the next moment. All we can do is act in our spheres of influence, which is so often about being available and loving to the next person

---

[24]Spencer LaJoye, "Take Ten: How Long," May 26, 2022, video, 10:05, www.youtube.com/watch?v=kG6OY3IY6Ik.
[25]LaJoye, "Take Ten: How Long."

we encounter. I'm in the choir and I turn to your music—both listening and singing it myself—to move all this through so I can keep going. I'm deeply grateful.

Spencer seems to have drawn a group of like-minded creatives and musicians who are committed to using music and art to make meaning around challenging experiences and social issues.

This small online community is characterized by appreciation of shared music, as well as some degree of similar religious experience or commitments (given Spencer's previous connections to American evangelical Christianity and frequent discussions of religious trauma). This Patreon community is also shaped by practices of silence, mindfulness, and embodiment. These rhythms of stillness affect patrons' physical, mental, and emotional states, and provide space for reflecting on faith, healing, and creativity. A patron named SL posted the following comment on another of Spencer's take ten videos: "Taking the time to watch your video this AM has healed a piece of me for the long road ahead. Thank you. [prayer hands emoji] [red heart emoji]."[26] Music and poetry feature prominently in this community's ethos, as Spencer and their patrons share a passion for art and a belief in the potential of creativity to lead toward positive change.

CULTIVATING CHURCH COMMUNITY ONLINE

Each of these examples of online community formation shows how meaningful experiences of connection, support, and transformation can happen across a wide range of digitally mediated forms. Communities can form online through polished presentations or informal home videos. There is no one way for people to connect, and churches need not feel pressured to measure up to some external standard of what "good" online communal practices or worship necessarily look like. At the same time, taking the approach of simply livestreaming "what we've always done" is unlikely to be effective or meaningful. Instead, churches and church leaders have an opportunity to reflect on what is important to them and their worshiping communities, what resources they have access to, and what platform(s) may be

---

[26]Spencer LaJoye, "Take Ten: Trans Day of Visibility!," April 1, 2022, www.patreon.com/posts/take-ten-trans-64541002.

most accessible and appropriate, given the unique affordances of each form of digital media.

In his contribution to *The Distanced Church: Reflections on Doing Church Online*, Arni Svanur Danielsson writes compellingly on this theme:

> The key questions churches are faced with at this juncture are not how they can become experts at streaming video over the Internet, nor are they about how many cameras will be needed, or what kind of microphones, lights or video mixers. Instead, on a fundamental level, the question is about the use of a new medium and how it can nurture and strengthen the connection with and between the members of a faith community or parish. It is about how this medium can facilitate participation that empowers a faith community to witness rather than merely watch a worship service.[27]

The good news is that the church has always been in the process of adapting to new media technologies, and the same has been true within the last several years. There are multiple forms of media that have become comfortable for us, and still more that offer new possibilities for the future. Each of these media has its own affordances; a Facebook livestream provides unique opportunities that a Zoom call does not, and vice versa. Apps such as Instagram, TikTok, Be Real, and Marco Polo allow for different forms of online communication and sharing. Each digital platform also has limitations. A stream with a text chat may be able to accommodate more people interacting at once than a Zoom call, but it does facilitate a kind of interaction that is more distant from in-person conversation.

When I interviewed Pete Phillips over Zoom, he described some of the advantages and disadvantages of various platforms. Phillips particularly contrasts the affordances of a Zoom meeting with those of a YouTube stream. Referring to human capacities for awareness of and empathy toward others, Phillips remarks:

> And indeed, they're enhanced a bit more because whereas if you're in a . . . church of about thirty people, you won't really look at them. . . . But if you're in a Zoom meeting of thirty people, you're forced to look at them. You're forced to see every single movement that they make. And your eyes are attracted to

---

[27] Arni Svanur Danielsson, "Connection Trumps Technology," in *The Distanced Church: Reflections on Doing Church Online*, ed. Heidi Campbell (n.p.: Digital Religion, 2020), 11, https://doi.org/10.21423/distancedchurch.

all the body language that they're exuding. And in a way that can be very negative, because that means you get Zoom fatigue. And the early encephalography around that suggests the brain is heating up all the time because it's trying to monitor everything, everybody's body language. And it's not good. So that means that classes or church, what have you, do need to be shorter than normal because otherwise you're going to be frying people's brains."[28]

Zoom interactions can actually facilitate a high degree of social engagement and felt community. There can be greater "face-to-face" interaction between groups of a certain size than even in person, as it is possible to see and register the facial expressions of multiple people simultaneously. Phillips sees the potential of this intensity in addition to its problems. He argues that "we overread the kind of situations that we're in" but also are much more connected to those people than we typically would be in a church service, with everyone seated facing forward. A platform such as Zoom introduces a "church in the round" kind of dynamic, in which we see other people as they sing, pray, and react to the statements and actions of others. Phillips contends that this is "a much more kind of integrated and communal experience than some of our churches are. And you could say therefore it's more real than physical church."[29]

Using the affordances of Zoom responsibly, then, may involve a greater awareness of the mental and emotional weight of the platform, which led to the familiar symptoms of "Zoom fatigue" in the early stages of the pandemic. When so many interactions and meetings took place in this medium, our brains were being bombarded with more information at once than we were accustomed to. However, the medium can be used effectively to allow for meaningful connections that are also informed by awareness of the impact on people's energy and mental state.

Contrasted with Zoom, Phillips also sees particular possibilities and limitations in streaming platforms such as YouTube. Phillips notes that universities are becoming aware that students experience any media they encounter on YouTube as entertainment, which inflects their learning while on the platform. He suggests that churches are beginning to see value in having online pastors in digital media environments to direct or facilitate the experience of online participants. This is even more necessary on YouTube or

---

[28] Peter Phillips, interview by author, Zoom, March 1, 2023.
[29] Phillips, interview.

another streaming video platform, because while participation through the chat box is possible, it requires a degree of guidance, even coaching and modeling what is being asked of them. Phillips imagines how an "online pastor" could help to curate and facilitate engagement with a streamed service in a model similar to previous versions of religious variety shows on radio and television. In Phillips's view, this would "make the most of YouTube's entertainment model," while also having a host online who could guide the liturgy. Phillips acknowledges that this platform will tend toward passive audiences (though he notes, "That can be okay because some churches are passive"). Overall, Phillips suggests, "You have to adapt the way you do church . . . for the various media that you use. Zoom is the one we think is the most communal. Whereas YouTube is more entertainment based and therefore more difficult to engage communitarianly."[30]

Phillips also acknowledges the limitations of Zoom. While it is well suited to communal interaction, it is not well suited to communal music: "Zoom technology and the company needed to go in different direction on sound. And so music, corporate singing is impossible on Zoom because of the way they buffer sound across different spaces differently. I think that they could solve it, but they haven't. They've chosen not to. And I think that means that corporate singing is really hard."[31]

Even so, Phillips has also encountered meaningful expressions of music in online worship through Zoom. In a Zoom meeting led by a worship leader singing and playing piano, with the participants muted, it was still possible to see other worshipers participating, though the auditory experience was limited. In this case, the worship leader used the music as an invitation to prayer and reflection, leading to communal sharing. Phillips found this experience "absolutely brilliant . . . just to be . . . invited to listen to the music and allow the Spirit to work within us. And then people came back with some of the same kinds of prayers and words that God had given them." The participants in this Zoom worship meeting felt a spiritual connection to each other through the prayers and reflections inspired by the shared music despite the distance between them and the different perspectives represented in the group.[32]

---

[30]Phillips, interview.
[31]Phillips, interview.
[32]Phillips, interview.

The audio delay on Zoom is a barrier to typical expressions of musical worship, but it does not preclude meaningful experiences involving music in community. And the arrival of new technologies does not necessarily make older media obsolete. Phillips describes an expression of shared singing that arose within a very small church in the rural areas in the north of the United Kingdom:

> They only had about two or three members. And so occasionally they got used to doing telephone conferences with one another, on the landlines that they had. Then when lockdown came, a few other people in villages nearby heard about this and said, "Can we join you in your telephone conference?" So they eventually got about twelve people phoning into this telephone conference, and then they realized they could sing hymns with one another because the telephone network doesn't have the delays that Zoom has. And so they found that they were singing together and building one another up. And it was fantastic. And using this old-time technology, you know, a landline . . . so when the lockdown stopped, they carried on and they began to grow even larger. So . . . using the right technology . . . allow[ed] sung music to really buzz.[33]

The question that our churches face is not, "Is this or that expression of digitally mediated worship feasible or legitimate?" Instead, the question can be, "What forms of technology and expressions of liturgy can be successfully combined, given the resources we have?"

In his chapter "Lockdown Ecclesiologies: The Limits and Possibilities of Enforced Online First Expressions," Steve Taylor contends that each platform's limitations can become generative of new imaginative possibilities. Working within constraints can allow creativity to flourish. Taylor points out that digital media has facilitated "new ways to conceive materiality and visibility" in our online interactions and also "ways of redefining the public square." He notes that ministry practitioners were beginning to experience online community as "a legitimate and singular public space where people meet, share, inspire and offer to help one another."[34] In this chapter, I have described several online communities that allow for just these kinds of interactions.

We should not be too quick to dismiss online expressions of church in their earliest stages. Taylor argues that dismissive judgments of digital communities, especially in the church (which has not been particularly experienced

---

[33]Phillips, interview.
[34]Taylor, "Lockdown Ecclesiologies," 158-59.

in building this kind of community), would be premature: "Comparing first expressions of enforced online formation with the long experiences of face-to-face expressions of church is like comparing the first flight of the Wright brothers with a first-class crossing of the Atlantic."[35] Even despite many churches' lack of experience, those first expressions were at times very meaningful. Zach Lambert, a pastor in Austin, Texas, encountered some of these meaningful expressions at the very beginning of the pandemic:

> The first Sunday, we had over 200 comments during the livestream. The second Sunday, over 400 comments. The majority of those 600 comments had nothing to do with the music, the message, the announcements, or any other content coming through the screen. People were talking to each other; they were greeting each other by name and checking on each other.
> "Hi fam"
> "Buenos días!"
> "Sending virtual hugs to you."
> "How's that sweet little boy doing?"
> "Can't wait to hang out with you again when this is all over!!!"
> "Congratulations to the newlyweds"
> "How's the pregnancy going? How are you feeling?"
> "Has your job been affected?"
> "Can we send you guys dinner this week?"
> They were even typing in greetings from their kids to other kids whose parents were on the chat. I was stunned.[36]

Lambert goes on to exhort the church to value "connection over content." He encourages churches to embrace the responsibility to "intentionally create spaces where deep friendship can blossom." Doing ministry online can be intimidating; but as Lambert reminds us, "No matter how great we are, there will always be someone who has better and more compelling content than we do. But there is one thing each of us can offer that no one else can: connection with our unique church family."[37]

Connection is paramount. The goal of the church in this new landscape is not to win at the attention economy or to bend the algorithms of social media

---

[35] Taylor, "Lockdown Ecclesiologies," 168.
[36] Zach W. Lambert, "Facilitating Deep Friendships Digitally When Analog Acquaintances Are Gone," in Campbell, *Distanced Church*, 19-20.
[37] Lambert, "Facilitating Deep Friendships," 21.

to God's will; it is to learn to live and love well in a world that has been transformed by online media and is continuing to change. Phillips suggests a helpful stance of humility and curiosity for the church as we move forward with this task:

> The younger you are, the more likely you are actually to understand the tech and do it properly. I'm in my late fifties, but most of the people, the majority, in my church are seventy-plus. And so, there's this big gap down to the twenty-, thirty-year-olds. And how are we going to embrace them, how are we going to embrace their use of tech, because they're way ahead? How do you worship God through TikTok? Would you even want to? And to some extent [this is] the place where we need to be going with technology and worship and everything: What are the youngsters doing? What is Gen Z doing?[38]

Phillips's openness to younger generations, particularly in following their lead when it comes to technology, is a refreshingly welcome stance for church leaders and thinkers to emulate. DJ Soto offers a similar invitation to the church, highlighting the struggles that some leaders from previous generations are experiencing when considering the potential of online and metaverse worship. Soto sees a resistance and reluctance, with churches being pulled "kicking and screaming into this new technology." He is sympathetic to churches that only recently adopted and adapted to things such as having a website, social media profile, or livestream, that now feel pressured to learn yet more new approaches and ways to connect. Soto wonders whether for some church leaders this may be too much to ask.[39]

Contrasted with this, Soto offers a hopeful vision of what the next generation of Christian leaders bring to these new challenges:

> But the younger generation gets it, the younger thinkers get it. They were birthed in Minecraft servers and Fortnite interactions and V-bucks, and their economics, their connections, their relationships are already in some form of what the metaverse is. So it doesn't even faze them. The next gen of church planters are going to go crazy once they get into it, because they're not hesitant. They're not reluctant. There [are] no theological qualms for them. Even if they got past the theological qualms, you see, the technological aptitude of these senior leaders, even for online pastors, [is] still a step or two behind. But

---

[38] Phillips, interview.
[39] DJ Soto, interview by author, Zoom, January 13, 2023.

these—and this is [used as] a derogatory term, but I don't think it is—these gamer kids are going to kill it when it comes to Web 3.0 church planting when the time comes. So I think there's another little nugget . . . to really empower the next gen, maybe even get out of their way, try to figure out how they can do that because they're going to take ministry to a whole other level from what they've been birthed in.[40]

It is not essential that the church use the most current technology or the newest social media platform; there is also value in familiarity and comfort for congregants whose learning curves may be greater. But the church may also have an opportunity to demonstrate respect and openness toward younger generations. Digital natives have much to offer the church, far beyond their technological experiences and aptitude, but those gifts around technology are valuable as well.

The church has much to learn as it finds its footing in a world shaped by digital media and the internet. Scholars and leaders have reflection to do on the implications of these new realities on our theology and practice. How will we grapple with questions of participation, embodiment, mediation, and virtuality? Will we continue using frameworks and formulations crafted in times when the world we now inhabit was nearly unimaginable? Or will we recognize the necessity of revisiting our patterns of practice and thought, acknowledging that, while they are familiar, comfortable, and meaningful, they are not perfect? Will we learn from communities and leaders who may not share our convictions but have begun to leverage media in powerfully effective ways?

---

[40]Soto, interview.

CONCLUSION

Where Did We Come From? Where Do We Go?

WITH THE ADVENT OF THE INTERNET, a technocultural revolution began, along with a dramatic reshaping of global economies. Human attention became a new frontier of colonization as corporations and online platforms began capitalizing on the susceptibility of the human brain to the dizzying stimulation and connectivity offered by these new technologies. At the same time, the internet became such a ubiquitous presence that it began to slowly edge toward becoming invisible. Like other technologies before it (including written language, architecture, and audiovisual media), at some point the internet became, and in some contexts is still becoming, a completely normalized and assumed part of our lives. As we live in a world exploding with superfluous information, human attention is at a premium, and constant advertising and monetized distraction vie for our every waking moment. Justin E. H. Smith highlights the ways the attention economy jeopardizes our attention's use toward human flourishing and calls for a renewal of "transformative moral commitment."

Smith's framing resonates with Martin Buber's twin concepts of *I-It* and *I-Thou* relation. In a technological and mediated world built to distract and disconnect, Christian discipleship necessitates a return to spiritual depth and openness to transformation, whatever media may be involved in our relationships. The way forward for the church and for church music is not greater facility in competing within the attention economy. Our goal is not to become shinier, more impressive, and more likely to keep people from clicking away from our meticulously entertaining livestreams. Instead, we can seek out ways to utilize media technology that subvert the cultural norms of fragmentation and distraction, and invite us to greater awareness, depth, and connection.

If churches and church music scholars wish to engage meaningfully in conversation around online worship, there are certain topics that are important to address. Four pairs of opposing, dichotomous categories often appear in discussions of online and hybrid worship. An important part of developing nuanced and productive conversation around digitally mediated rituals is exploring the complexity of each of these categories. Participation is an important aspect of church music; however, church music, worship, and even faith itself move along the full spectrum from active to passive. Embodiment is a crucial part of a faith, based on the incarnation of God; however, the bodies of people using any number of technologies new and old are still present and significant. We may aspire to unmediated relations with God and each other; however, we must acknowledge that every part of our lives is mediated and instead find connection and immediacy in the midst of that mediation. We may be tempted to divide the virtual from the real, demonizing the former and idealizing the latter; however, we live in a world where these two spheres are closely overlapping and cannot be separated from each other. These categories are not reasons to shut down reflection or conversation about the potential of online and hybrid practices. Rather, they are areas for us to explore what it means to be human in a changing world.

The first dichotomy involves participation, with categories of active and passive featuring prominently in hesitations around integrating digital technology. *Sacrosanctum Concilium* has popularized the language of "fully conscious and active participation" as normative for worship. This is a helpful corrective from overly passive liturgy in which the laity has no active role. The goal of participation can also be seen in negotiations within evangelical worship concerts. Congregational participation becomes the essential alchemical ingredient that transmutes into worship what could otherwise be critiqued as performance (which, in evangelical framings of worship, would be negative). Rather than a reductive binary that considers activity good and passivity bad, I suggest that all liturgy does involve and should involve a mixture of active and passive experience. Interpassivity is a helpful category for conceptualizing this, as in worship we delegate or share not only the active tasks of offering worship to God but also more passive experiences of encountering or receiving God.

Conclusion

Interpassivity can also be seen in a variety of media forms, such as a sitcom with a laugh track, or a video game stream viewed by gamers who watch others play. Interpassivity can also be understood in theological terms related to Christian faith. Rather than placing a burden of participation and a duty to constant affective intensity on worshipers, worship leaders can acknowledge that there is a passive, receptive element to our faith and to God's revelation of love. We can rely on God's faithfulness, and the shared faith of our worshiping communities, rather than punishing ourselves with guilt for our affective shortcomings in worship.

The second dichotomy is often constructed around embodiment. Popular conversations around online worship often focus on embodiment as an essential quality of proximal worship that is assumed to be lacking in online expressions. However, our experiences of music making and even music listening are always embodied. Music and other elements of liturgical practice become part of our "body schemas," combinations of cultural norms and narratives and muscle memory that condition how we show up physically in the world. Learning musical skills is a form of embodiment, as we internalize a piece of technology (i.e., a musical instrument or technique) into our body schema. Our musical practices come to shape and define our bodies, expanding our sense of self to include those objects and behaviors. Even listening to music occurs through unavoidably embodied processes of simulation, and our bodies respond instinctually to musical sound as if we were participating in making it; our muscles and nerves react sympathetically with those of other musicians. We use our bodies to make sense of sound and experience it as music through behaviors such as subvocalization.

Another essential part of conversation about embodiment in worship is acknowledging that our normative patterns of worship do not actually value and include all bodies. Our churches have been complicit in ableist and exclusionary practices toward believers who experience embodiment in ways targeted by marginalization. It is not enough for us to claim that, because of the importance of embodiment, we must return to our habitual worship practices and structures from prior to the pandemic. Instead, we have a responsibility to restructure our life together while prioritizing those who have been excluded. The way forward will include a faithful reckoning with the physical contours of our practices and technologies (such as liturgies and architecture) and an integration of digital technologies that can allow greater participation and equity. Theologically speaking, human beings are always embodied, whatever media they are using. The bodily implications and impact of various practices do differ, but nothing we do is disembodied.

A third binary that appears in conversation around worship concerns mediation and the ideal of unmediated experience. The Christian music and worship industries have marketed their products to promise an unmediated encounter with the divine through the use of mass-produced media. They aspire to erase the presence of these mediators, hiding music, technology, and even worship leaders from view to imply that none of these media are a part of the believer's intimate encounter with God. However, all of Christian worship has always been mediated. Music itself can be understood as both a form of media and an act of mediation. A philosophy of "radical mediation" invites us to consider that our experience of the world and of relationships is not hindered by mediation but rather made possible by it. Immediacy happens in the midst of mediation. The Christian faith has always involved mediation, and we need not try to escape it. God has operated through all kinds of media, from the burning bush, to the temple, to the Bible, to the incarnation, to the ecclesial body of Christ.

The fourth dichotomy is between virtuality and reality. The distinction between "the real" and "the virtual" carries numerous implications and meanings that have shifted over time. Sometimes these implications have included an assumption of virtual spaces and experiences as unreal, false, or even leading to evil. However, as online technologies become more integrated into our society, these two spheres are overlapping more and more and are no longer practically separable. Additionally, there is an increasing body of compelling evidence that real and genuine moral formation can take place even in fully virtual environments. Recent studies and theological reflection suggest that the kinds of meaningful encounter we associate with "face-to-face" relationship are in fact possible through digital media and that these experiences can be personally transformative. Despite cultural stereotypes of virtual reality technologies as antisocial and malforming, the real experiences of virtual reality users suggest that the technology both is meaningfully social and can have moral impact in positive ways. Virtual reality is also a space where concertgoers and congregants alike have found meaningful

Conclusion

experiences, with both advantages and disadvantages compared to more traditional arrangements of these events.

Having discussed each of these four dichotomies, I suggest that a productive path forward would involve imagining and enacting a hybrid approach to music ministry. In a digitally mediatized world that is continuing to integrate online technologies as they become increasingly invisible to us, it will be necessary to reconceptualize music ministry as involving both online and offline expressions. This hybrid approach will acknowledge that the internet has become one of the "places" where we spend a significant portion of our time in daily life. Our discipleship and worship must include this aspect of life, not ignore or dismiss it as spiritually irrelevant or hopelessly depraved. Rather than trying to return "back to normal" before the significant changes brought on by the forced online transition during 2020, a hybrid approach to ministry and church music will acknowledge that both online and offline faith expressions must be integrated. Revisiting and clarifying the purposes of church music will provide a helpful compass in navigating this new landscape. Part of this challenge will be learning to use new technologies and media platforms in ways that are truly participatory, transformative, appropriate to the medium, and centered on God.

In the pursuit of learning these kinds of technological skills, I provided three case studies of online ritual communities. Our churches have much to learn about facilitating participatory and transformative communal expressions that make effective use of the affordances of various digital media. Whether through observing a community of gamers online who gather around Twitch.tv streams to share music, meaningful stories, personal support, and concerted action for justice; an audience of a popular podcast that engages in spiritual practices and shares insights and blessings and grief with one another; or a small community of supportive artists and music listeners on Patreon who are exploring how practices of creativity, embodiment, and encouragement can make a difference in a world full of hurt, Christian leaders, ministers, and scholars can look to these and other examples for evidence of what might be possible for hybrid churches.

The essential question is how churches can facilitate connection and community leading to Christian discipleship and worship, using the tools at their disposal that are appropriate to their contexts and goals. We need not be limited to any predetermined or prescriptive approach to digital media. There is no single platform that is right for every community. There are challenges and limitations to using these technologies for music in churches, but this does not need to mean we give up and decide that nothing can be done. Instead, our churches can lean in to the task of discerning what means may be appropriate to their context, what forms of ministry the Holy Spirit may be drawing them to embody, and the gifts of younger generations for forging connections in these new worlds.

MOVING FORWARD: SEEKING NEW CREATION IN A NEW MEDIA ENVIRONMENT

There remains much more to be done. The full implications of this digital revolution will not become clear for decades at least, perhaps over a century. The issues raised in this book will not be solved in my lifetime. However, at least three areas for further research and practical ministry are apparent.

First, there are now huge repositories of online church services available for digital ethnographic study. Since so many churches now have online services, researchers can have greater access to a wider geographic range of churches with fewer barriers around travel and logistics than ever before. There will also continue to be more online expressions of religious community appearing as church planters move into hybrid and metaverse spaces. Further research can be attentive to what is happening in these communities specifically, as well as broader demographic shifts that will doubtless continue. What are the characteristics of religious communities that meet only online or include hybrid elements while eschewing owning a traditional church building? What can we learn from these new expressions, on both micro and macro levels?

Second, there are new technologies and new media platforms appearing quickly. Zoom will not be the end of this evolution. There will be much more to learn about the affordances of these various platforms, which ones tend toward use patterns that are destructive, and which may have greater potential for meaningful ministry. A comparative study of the affordances of a variety of media platforms, along with their potential for facilitating collaborative and communal musicking, promises to be fascinating and productive. As one example, a platform such as TikTok has been used extensively for

Conclusion

collaborative music making, as users can layer harmonies, duets, and even larger instrumental and vocal ensembles to create compelling and impressive musical compilations. What might this look like in a church music context?

Third, while I have argued that categories of participation, embodiment, mediation, and virtuality are important in considering online and hybrid worship, my treatment of them is far from exhaustive. There are numerous other disciplines and reflections on local congregational ministry that could contribute meaningfully to this conversation, and delving deeper into one or more of these categories and accompanying theological implications seems likely to unearth further thought-provoking insights and intriguing possibilities.

Church music practitioners have encountered huge shifts, new questions, and unexpected obstacles to doing the work of music ministry with their congregations. There are also many fresh opportunities and promising potentials in the new expressions of community and music making that are emerging. Scholars within church music studies and related fields, pastors, and church musicians have the opportunity to engage meaningfully with this changing landscape, learning from each other and from faith leaders and communities. This book represents my contribution to that important conversation. I hope to offer useful reflections, understandings, and connections to people committed to the music of the church. We will not find our way in this new day alone; we need one another. Let the conversation continue.

APPENDIX

Live Chat Responses on ZeplaHQ's Twitch.tv Stream and YouTube Comments on Related Music Videos

DEMONSTRATING FEELINGS OF ANTICIPATION AND OWNERSHIP RELATED TO THE MUSIC

Shinjima: "the music is coming"
exp31: "oh man is it coming"
Shaggyshag10: "inc[oming] best song in the game"
Hatlebee: "here comes the song chat"
DefinitelyNotDelirious: "music about to carry"
Amantiso: "Here we go"
mettog: "best song doh"
glbozz: "It's time for the music"
Mr_Snuggle_: "the music god damn"
bigdirtyphil: "here it comes"
Zluzaya: "Now the song"
thatluckydash: "BGM [background music] TIME"
Forwards_of_Light: "HERE WE GO"
namath_0: "jam time"
hemlocckk: "[sad emoji] this music"
SixSixTrample: "the song is what gets you"
Wichher: "Song moment [purple heart emoji]"
RebootSam: "OUR SONG"
bigbad86: "THE MUSIC IS HERE AT LAST"
Forwards_of_Light: "I have this song on repeat all the time"
xeptix: "help I've been listening to this song on repeat for days"
Bi0_: "This song, I love this song more than any song in any video game ever."

DEMONSTRATING EMBODIED AND PARTICIPATORY RESPONSES TO DIGITALLY MEDIATED MUSIC

Alescha: "I'm not crying, you're crying"
Gyro_Zeppeli__: "who's cutting onions in chat"
Mr_Snuggle_: "somebody hold me"
RebootSam: "You're crying, I'm crying, everybody is crying"
OwlMoon: "@Mr_Snuggle_ I'll hold you"
thatluckydash: "@Mr_Snuggles_ can you hold me too please"
Zebrios: "Here comes the flood of tears [crying emoji]"
LankosBtw: "lets hold hands chat"
TrowGundam: "And I'm crying again"
guidodragon: "ahwww zepla big hug [purple heart emoji]"
mechanikatt: "tales of looooossss and fiiiiire and faaaaaate. . . ."
Gonzerido: "Tales of loss and fire and faith [crying emoji]"
Chitalian: "tails of loooooss and fiiiire and faaaith [catjam emoji]"
Kirilgheya: "Forge aheaaaaaaaaaaaaaaaaaaaaaad"
Monokerros: "TO T HE END"
bagel72: "Forge ahead to the end we pray [catjam emoji]"
shinxoe: "[catjam emoji] Forge ahead, till the end, we pray"

DEMONSTRATING A SENSE OF RE-EXPERIENCING THE STORY, INTERPASSIVE ENGAGEMENT

ephemerle: "doesn't hurt less the second time [crying emojis]"
aapyon: "[sad emoji] I can't"
Koikev: "I can't, not again"
ClockworkEffigy: "it was somehow more painful the second time viewing"
SimplePsyke: "never mind I already lost it playing through this last night, still hits so hard"
Kelvargaming: "**** man, even second time I'm in shambles"
Casardis: "my heart can't take it"

YOUTUBE COMMENTS CONNECTING TO THE COMPOSER'S LIFE STORY AND VIEWER'S LIFE EXPERIENCES

Zaiz_En: "Remember when we were all #WelcomebackSoken . . . and then he scores the expansion like this . . . what a Boss!"

Appendix

hoyhoy007: "We dont deserve Soken [crying emoji]"

Kong Chang: "I still can't believe Soken composed his best work from the hospital . . . #WelcomeBackSoken."

Whyspurful : "What makes this so much better, is [*Endwalker*'s] soundtrack was created in a hospital. The composer if you guys remember was battling cancer. And he made these masterpieces while literally dying. So happy hes in remission, true strength."

Matt Smillie: "nothing sounds more like 'growing hope' than this [music]!"

Erd Nuzz: "I was strong, didnt get too emotional to carry on. Until this music started in its full glory. I've couldnt control my tears and everything broke in that moment and i was just a pure raw wave of emotions. I love this song."

Gystiel: "Almost cried my eyes out playing through this. . . . It's been a whole month since I finished [*Endwalker*], still can't listen to this song without tearing up."

Holly Montalvo: "I feel super emotional whenever I hear this song, and I'm not sure if it's because of the song itself, because I was a sobbing mess the first time I heard the complete version of it, or both. Probably both [to be honest]"

Miroslav Kyurkchiev: "For someone who suffers with depression, I was able to relate to this whole storyline so much."

Dundun: "Having just recently lost my mother, and with me being genuinely aimless in my life without her, I came back to this vid. The lyrics hit even harder now."

Foul Beast: "I had a smile on my face all the way through this . . . even at the parts where everyone else was crying, for a personal reason . . .

". . . There was a line from Ghosts of Tsushima [another video game] that helped me put the loss of my father behind me. 'Your father is the wind at your back.' It really stuck with me, to the point where things that some people see as burdens, I see as a kind of driving force. So as worried as I was after we found out what happened to [two other characters in the *Endwalker* story], the moment that wind blew through, I knew it was all gonna work out.

"Walk on, never look back.

"Through you, we live. :)"

Bibliography

Adorno, Theodor W. *Essays on Music*. Translated by Susan H. Gillespie. Berkeley: University of California Press, 2002.

Agee, Richard J. "The Printed Dissemination of the Roman Gradual in Italy During the Early Modern Period." *Notes* 64, no. 1 (2007): 9-42.

Ammerman, Nancy Tatom. "Religious Identities and Religious Narratives." In *Handbook of the Sociology of Religion*, edited by Michele Dillon, 207-24. Cambridge: Cambridge University Press, 2003.

Apostolidis, Paul. *Stations of the Cross: Adorno and Christian Right Radio*. Durham, NC: Duke University Press, 2000.

Barz, Gregory F., and Timothy J. Cooley. *Shadows in the Field: New Perspectives for Fieldwork in Ethnomusicology*. 2nd ed. New York: Oxford University Press, 2008.

Berger, Teresa. "Digital Devotion: Christianity Online." In *The Quadcast*, October 11, 2017. Podcast, 22:00. https://soundcloud.com/yaleuniversity/the-quadcast-digital-devotion-christianity-online.

———. *@ Worship: Liturgical Practices in Digital Worlds*. Liturgy, Worship, and Society. New York: Routledge, 2018.

Bernstein, Jane A. "The House of Scotto: A Printing Dynasty." In *Music Printing in Renaissance Venice: The Scotto Press (1539–1572)*, 29-54. New York: Oxford University Press, 1998.

———. "Publish or Perish? Palestrina and Print Culture in 16th-Century Italy." *Early Music* 35, no. 2 (May 2007): 225-35.

Best, Harold M. *Music Through the Eyes of Faith*. San Francisco: HarperSanFrancisco, 1993.

Born, Georgina. "On Musical Mediation: Ontology, Technology and Creativity." *Twentieth-Century Music* 2, no. 1 (2005): 7-36.

Born, Georgina, and Andrew Barry. "Music, Mediation Theories and Actor-Network Theory." *Contemporary Music Review* 37, no. 5/6 (October 2018): 443-87.

Born, Georgina, and Christopher Haworth. "Music and Intermediality After the Internet: Aesthetics, Materialities and Social Forms." In *Music and Digital Media: A Planetary Anthropology*, edited by Georgina Born, 378-438. London: UCL Press, 2022.

Bradley, C. Randall. *From Memory to Imagination: Reforming the Church's Music*. Grand Rapids, MI: Eerdmans, 2012.

Bryant, Gregory. "Rhythm and the Body." In *A Multidisciplinary Approach to Embodiment: Understanding Human Being*, edited by Nancy Kimberly Dess, 65-70. New York: Routledge, 2021.

Buber, Martin. *I and Thou*. New York: Scribner, 1958.

Burnham, Bo. "Welcome to the Internet—Bo Burnham (from 'Inside'—ALBUM OUT NOW)." June 4, 2021. Video, 4:40. www.youtube.com/watch?v=k1BneeJTDcU.

Busman, Joshua Kalin. "(Re)Sounding Passion: Listening to American Evangelical Worship Music, 1997-2015." PhD diss., University of North Carolina at Chapel Hill, 2015.

Campbell, Heidi A. *Digital Religion: Understanding Religious Practice in New Media Worlds*. New York: Routledge, 2013.

———, ed. *The Distanced Church: Reflections on Doing Church Online*. N.p.: Digital Religion, 2020. https://doi.org/10.21423/distancedchurch.

———. *Exploring Religious Community Online: We Are One in the Network*. Digital Formations 24. New York: Peter Lang, 2005.

———. "Understanding the Relationship Between Religion Online and Offline in a Networked Society." *Journal of the American Academy of Religion* 80, no. 1 (2012): 64-93.

Campbell, Heidi A., and Wendi Bellar. *Digital Religion: The Basics*. London: Routledge, 2022.

Campbell, Heidi A., and Michael W. DeLashmutt. "Studying Technology and Ecclesiology in Online Multi-site Worship." *Journal of Contemporary Religion* 29, no. 2 (2014): 267-85.

Campbell, Heidi A., and John Dyer, eds. *Ecclesiology for a Digital Church*. London: SCM Press, 2022.

Chandler, Daniel, and Rod Munday. *A Dictionary of Media and Communication*. Oxford: Oxford University Press, 2020.

Cherry, Constance M. *The Music Architect: Blueprints for Engaging Worshipers in Song*. Grand Rapids, MI: Baker Academic, 2016.

Cheruvallil-Contractor, Sariya, and Suha Shakkour. *Digital Methodologies in the Sociology of Religion*. New York: Bloomsbury Academic, 2016.

Chicka, Benjamin J. *Playing as Others: Theology and Ethical Responsibility in Video Games*. Waco, TX: Baylor University Press, 2021.

Child Mind Institute. "Self Esteem in the Age of Social Media." January 19, 2019. Video, 55:35. www.youtube.com/watch?v=UmUm7oBqCVw.

Conrades, George. "The Future of the Internet: Predicting the Unpredictable." In *The Internet*, ed. Gray Young, 179-87. The Reference Shelf 70. New York: H. W. Wilson, 1998.

Cook, Deborah, ed. *Theodor Adorno Key Concepts*. Stocksfield, UK: Acumen, 2008.

Cook, Nicholas. "Digital Technology and Cultural Practice." In *The Cambridge Companion to Music in Digital Culture*, edited by Nicholas Cook, Monique Marie Ingalls, and David Trippett, 5-28. New York: Cambridge University Press, 2019.

Cook, Nicholas, Monique Marie Ingalls, and David Trippett, eds. *The Cambridge Companion to Music in Digital Culture*. New York: Cambridge University Press, 2019.

Bibliography

Cooley, Timothy J., Katherine Meizel, and Nasir Syed. "Virtual Fieldwork." In *Shadows in the Field: New Perspectives for Fieldwork in Ethnomusicology*, 2nd ed., ed. Gregory F. Barz and Timothy J. Cooley, 90-107. New York: Oxford University Press, 2008.

Cooper, Anthony-Paul, Samuli Laato, Suvi Nenonen, Nicolas Pope, David Tjiharuka, and Erkki Sutinen. "The Reconfiguration of Social, Digital and Physical Presence: From Online Church to Church Online." *Hervormde Teologiese Studies* 77, no. 3 (2021): e1-9.

Cooper, Martin, and Kirsty Macaulay. "Contemporary Christian Radio in Britain: A New Genre on the National Dial." *Radio Journal* 13, no. 1-2 (2015): 75-87.

Cooper-White, Pamela. "Intersubjectivity." In *Encyclopedia of Psychology and Religion*, edited by David A. Leeming, 882-86. Boston: Springer, 2014.

Cusic, Don. *Encyclopedia of Contemporary Christian Music Pop, Rock, and Worship*. Santa Barbara, CA: Greenwood, 2010.

Danielsson, Arni Svanur. "Connection Trumps Technology." In *The Distanced Church: Reflections on Doing Church Online*, edited by Heidi Campbell, 10-11. N.p.: Digital Religion, 2020. https://doi.org/10.21423/distancedchurch.

Dawn, Marva J. *Reaching Out Without Dumbing Down: A Theology of Worship for the Turn-of-the-Century Culture*. Grand Rapids, MI: Eerdmans, 1995.

Deleuze, Gilles, and Paul Bove. *Foucault*. Translated by Sean Hand. Minneapolis: University of Minnesota Press, 1988.

Delwiche, Aaron Alan, and Jennifer Jacobs Henderson. *The Participatory Cultures Handbook*. New York: Routledge, 2013.

DeNora, Tia. *Music-in-Action: Selected Essays in Sonic Ecology*. Ashgate Contemporary Thinkers on Critical Musicology. Farnham, UK: Ashgate, 2011.

———. *Music in Everyday Life*. Cambridge: Cambridge University Press, 2000.

Dorsett, Lyle W. *Billy Sunday and the Redemption of Urban America*. Grand Rapids, MI: Eerdmans, 1991.

Dosi, Giovanni, Alfonso Gambardella, Luigi Orsanigo, and Louis Galambos. *The Third Industrial Revolution in Global Business*. Comparative Perspectives in Business History. Cambridge: Cambridge University Press, 2013.

Dueck, Jonathan. *Congregational Music, Conflict, and Community*. Congregational Music Studies. London: Routledge, 2017.

Egliston, Ben. "Visions of the Material Body: Twitch.Tv and Post-Phenomenology." *Journal of Gaming & Virtual Worlds* 12, no. 3 (2020): 241-57.

Elvy, Peter, and Jerusalem Trust. *Opportunities and Limitations in Religious Broadcasting*. Edinburgh: Centre for Theology and Public Issues, 1991.

Erickson, Hal. *Religious Radio and Television in the United States, 1921–1991: The Programs and Personalities*. Jefferson, NC: McFarland, 1992.

"FACT 2020 Survey Results." *Faith Communities Today*. October 25, 2019. https://faithcommunitiestoday.org/fact-2020-survey/.

Farnsworth, Brandon. *Curating Contemporary Music Festivals: A New Perspective on Music's Mediation*. Music and Sound Culture 47. Bielefeld, Germany: Transcript, 2020.

Frandsen, Mary E. "Matters of Taste: The Lutheran Market for Sacred Music in the Seventeenth Century." *Early Music History* 39 (October 2020): 149-218.

Fuad, Chelcent. "The Practice of the Lord's Supper in 1 Corinthians 11:17-34 as a Socioreligious Ritual Failure." *Expository Times* 130, no. 5 (2019): 202-14.

Gault, Erika D. "'My People Are Free!': Theorizing the Digital Black Church." *Fire!!!* 6, no. 1 (2020): 1-16.

Gekker, Alex. "Let's Not Play: Interpassivity as Resistance in 'Let's Play' Videos." *Journal of Gaming & Virtual Worlds* 10, no. 3 (2018): 219-42.

Gerety, Finnian M. M. "Digital Guru: Embodiment, Technology, and the Transmission of Traditional Knowledge in Kerala." *Asian Ethnology* 77, no. 1/2 (2018): 3-32.

Gibson, James J. *The Senses Considered as Perceptual Systems*. Boston: Houghton Mifflin, 1966.

Gorrell, Angela. *Always On: Practicing Faith in a New Media Landscape*. Theology for the Life of the World. Grand Rapids, MI: Baker Academic, 2019.

———. "Gorrell Guide to Creating Online, Participatory Worship Services." N.d.

Grant, August E., Amanda F. C. Sturgill, Chiung Hwang Chen, and Daniel A. Stout. *Religion Online: How Digital Technology Is Changing the Way We Worship and Pray*. Santa Barbara, CA: Praeger, 2019.

Grusin, Richard. "Radical Mediation." *Critical Inquiry* 42, no. 1 (2015): 124-48.

Gur, Golan. "Body, Forces, and Paths: Metaphor and Embodiment in Jean-Philippe Rameau's Conceptualization of Tonal Space." *Music Theory Online* 14, no. 1 (2008). https://mtosmt.org/issues/mto.08.14.1/mto.08.14.1.gur.html.

Guthrie, Kate. *The Art of Appreciation: Music and Middlebrow Culture in Modern Britain*. California Studies in 20th-Century Music 30. Oakland: University of California Press, 2021

Hart, Michael, and Maxwell Fuller. *A Brief History of the Internet the Bright Side: The Dark Side*. Champaign, IL: Project Gutenberg, 1998.

Hatmaker, Jen. "Is the Church Dead? A Millennial's Perspective on Religion with Casper ter Kuile." *For the Love*, April 12, 2022. Podcast, 1:05:20. www.youtube.com/watch?v=WEPyYdjqs70.

Haugen, Marty. "All Are Welcome." Chicago: GIA Publications, Inc., 1994.

Heft, Harry. "Perceptual Information of 'An Entirely Different Order': The 'Cultural Environment' in the Senses Considered as Perceptual Systems." *Ecological Psychology* 29, no. 2 (2017): 122-45.

Hennion, Antoine. "Loving Music: From a Sociology of Mediation to a Pragmatics of Taste." *Comunicar* 17, no. 34 (2010): 25-33.

Herrera, Fernanda. "Virtual Embodiment and Embodied Cognition: Effect of Virtual Reality Perspective Taking Tasks on Empathy and Prejudice." In *A Multidisciplinary*

Approach to Embodiment: Understanding Human Being, ed. Nancy Kimberly Dess, 127-32. New York: Routledge, 2021.

Hillis, Ken. *Digital Sensations: Space, Identity, and Embodiment in Virtual Reality*. Electronic Mediations 1. Minneapolis: University of Minnesota Press, 1999.

Hodson, Richard. "Digital Revolution." *Nature* 563, no. 7733 (2018): S131.

Hoover, Stewart M. *Mass Media Religion: The Social Sources of the Electronic Church*. Newbury Park, CA: Sage, 1988.

Horsfield, Peter G. *Religious Television: The American Experience*. New York: Longman, 1984.

Howe, Blake, Stephanie Jensen-Moulton, Neil Lerner, and Joseph Straus. *The Oxford Handbook of Music and Disability Studies*. Oxford Handbooks in Music. Oxford: University Press, 2015.

Howe, Walt. "A Brief History of the Internet." In *The Internet*, ed. Gray Young, 3-7. The Reference Shelf 70. New York: H. W. Wilson, 1998.

Hustad, Don. *Jubilate II: Church Music in Worship and Renewal*. Carol Stream, IL: Hope, 1993.

———. *True Worship: Reclaiming the Wonder and Majesty*. Wheaton, IL: H. Shaw, 1998.

Ingalls, Monique Marie. "Awesome in This Place: Sound, Space, and Identity in Contemporary North American Evangelical Worship." PhD diss., University of Pennsylvania, 2008.

———. *Singing the Congregation: How Contemporary Worship Music Forms Evangelical Community*. New York: Oxford University Press, 2018.

———. "Worship on Screen: Building Networked Congregations Through Audiovisual Worship Media." In *Singing the Congregation: How Contemporary Worship Music Forms Evangelical Community*, 172-206. New York: Oxford University Press, 2018.

IntelligentHQ. "What Is the Digital Revolution?" Newstex, April 15, 2022. www.proquest.com/docview/2650270031/citation/9F63948C315949B5PQ/1.

"Is Online Worship as Good as It Seems?" The Network: Christian Reformed Church, July 29, 2020. https://network.crcna.org/topic/worship/general-worship/online-worship-good-it-seems.

Jones, Carys Wyn. *The Rock Canon: Canonical Values in the Reception of Rock Albums*. Ashgate Popular and Folk Music Series. Aldershot, UK: Ashgate, 2008.

Jones, James W. *Living Religion: Embodiment, Theology, and the Possibility of a Spiritual Sense*. New York: Oxford University Press, 2019.

Jones, Nona J. *From Social Media to Social Ministry: A Guide to Digital Discipleship*. Grand Rapids, MI: Zondervan, 2020.

Jones, Phil. *Virtual Reality Methods: A Guide for Researchers in the Social Sciences and Humanities*. Bristol, UK: Polity, 2022.

Jun, Guichun. "Virtual Reality Church as a New Mission Frontier in the Metaverse: Exploring Theological Controversies and Missional Potential of Virtual Reality Church." *Transformation* 37, no. 4 (2020): 297-305.

Kassabian, Anahid. *Ubiquitous Listening: Affect, Attention, and Distributed Subjectivity.* Berkeley: University of California Press, 2013.

Kelman, Ari Y. *Shout to the Lord: Making Worship Music in Evangelical America.* North American Religions. New York: New York University Press, 2018.

Kenny, Amy. *My Body Is Not a Prayer Request: Disability Justice in the Church.* Grand Rapids, MI: Baker Books, 2022.

Kernighan, Brian W. *Understanding the Digital World: What You Need to Know About Computers, the Internet, Privacy, and Security.* Princeton, NJ: Princeton University Press, 2017.

Kim, Youn, and Sander L. Gilman, eds. *The Oxford Handbook of Music and the Body.* Oxford Handbooks Online. New York: Oxford University Press, 2018.

Klaver, Miranda. *This Is My Desire: A Semiotic Perspective on Conversion in an Evangelical Seeker Church and a Pentecostal Church in the Netherlands.* Amsterdam: Pallas, 2011.

———. "Worship Music as Aesthetic Domain of Meaning and Bonding: The Glocal Context of a Dutch Pentecostal Church." In *The Spirit of Praise: Music and Worship in Global Pentecostal-Charismatic Christianity*, edited by Monique Marie Ingalls and Amos Yong, 97-132. University Park: Pennsylvania State University Press, 2015.

Korte, Martin. "The Impact of the Digital Revolution on Human Brain and Behavior: Where Do We Stand?" *Dialogues in Clinical Neuroscience* 22, no. 2 (2020): 101-11.

Krogh, Mads. "A Beat Is a Hybrid: Mediation, ANT and Music as Material Practice." *Contemporary Music Review* 37, no. 5-6 (2018): 529-53.

Kuile, Casper ter. *The Power of Ritual: Turning Everyday Activities into Soulful Practices.* New York: HarperOne, 2020.

LaJoye, Spencer. "Spencer LaJoye Is Creating Music and Sacred Space." Patreon. Accessed May 7, 2022. www.patreon.com/spencerlajoye.

———. "Take Ten: How Long." May 26, 2022. Video, 10:05. www.youtube.com/watch?v=kG6OY31Y6Ik.

———. "Take Ten: Trans Day of Visibility!" April 1, 2022. www.patreon.com/posts/take-ten-trans-64541002.

Lambert, Zach W. "Facilitating Deep Friendships Digitally When Analog Acquaintances Are Gone." In *The Distanced Church: Reflections on Doing Church Online*, edited by Heidi Campbell, 19-21. N.p.: Digital Religion, 2020.

Lanham, Richard A. *The Economics of Attention: Style and Substance in the Age of Information.* Chicago: University of Chicago Press, 2006.

Lemley, David. *Becoming What We Sing: Formation Through Contemporary Worship Music.* Grand Rapids, MI: Eerdmans, 2021.

Lévinas, Emmanuel. *Otherwise than Being, or, Beyond Essence.* Pittsburgh: Duquesne University Press, 1998.

Linderman, Alf. *The Reception of Religious Television: Social Semeiology Applied to an Empirical Case Study.* Acta Universitatis Upsaliensis, Psychologia et Sociologia Religionum 12. Uppsala: S. Academiae Ubsaliensis, 1996.

Bibliography

Lochte, Robert H. *Christian Radio: The Growth of a Mainstream Broadcasting Force*. Jefferson, NC: McFarland, 2006.

Mackie, Carolyn J. "Believing for Me: Žižek, Interpassivity, and Christian Experience." Paper presented at Institute for Christian Studies, May 2, 2013.

Margulis, Elizabeth Hellmuth. *On Repeat: How Music Plays the Mind*. New York: Oxford University Press, 2014.

Margulis, Elizabeth H., Patrick C. M. Wong, Cara Turnbull, Benjamin M. Kubit, and J. Devin McAuley. "Narratives Imagined in Response to Instrumental Music Reveal Culture-Bounded Intersubjectivity." *Proceedings of the National Academy of Sciences of the United States of America* 119, no. 4 (January 2022): e2110406119.

"Masayoshi Soken—Close in the Distance (FFXIV Ultima Thule Variations Fan Mix) [EW SPOILERS]." Simshadows, December 25, 2021. Video, 10:48. www.youtube.com/watch?v=7V1Mr7SpHew.

McAnally, Ken, and Guy Wallis. "Visual-Haptic Integration, Action and Embodiment in Virtual Reality." *Psychological Research* 86, no. 6 (2021): 1847-57.

"Metaverse Board—VR Church in the Metaverse." VR MMO Church, accessed May 24, 2023. www.vrchurch.org/board.

Miller, Kiri. *Playing Along: Digital Games, YouTube, and Virtual Performance*. New York: Oxford University Press, 2012.

Montague, Eugene. "Entrainment and Embodiment in Musical Performance." In *The Oxford Handbook of Music and the Body*, ed. Youn Kim and Sander L. Gilman, 177-92. Oxford: Oxford University Press, 2019.

Music, David W. "Bach or Rock: The Training of Church Musicians." *The American Organist* 46, no. 11 (2012): 58-66.

Myrick, Nathan. *Music for Others: Care, Justice, and Relational Ethics in Christian Music*. London: Oxford University Press, 2021.

Nadeem, Reem. "2. Projecting U.S. Religious Groups' Population Shares by 2070." Pew Research Center, September 13, 2022. https://www.pewresearch.org/religion/2022/09/13/projecting-u-s-religious-groups-population-shares-by-2070/.

Nakamura, Mia. "Music Sociology Meets Neuroscience." In *The Oxford Handbook of Music and the Body*, ed. Youn Kim and Sander L. Gilman, 127-42. Oxford: Oxford University Press, 2019.

Nekola, Anna E. "Introduction: Worship Media as Media Form and Mediated Practice: Theorizing the Intersections of Media, Music and Lived Religion." In *Congregational Music-Making and Community in a Mediated Age*, edited by Anna E. Nekola and Thomas Wagner, 1-21. Farnham, UK: Routledge, 2015.

Nekola, Anna E., and Thomas Wagner, eds. *Congregational Music-Making and Community in a Mediated Age*. Ashgate Congregational Music Studies. Farnham, UK: Routledge, 2015.

Noll, Mark A. *Turning Points: Decisive Moments in the History of Christianity*. 2nd ed. Grand Rapids, MI: Baker Books, 2000.

O'Brien, Sarah. "Playing the Zombie: Participation and Interpassivity in Gothic XR." *Body, Space & Technology Journal* 19, no. 1 (2020): 76-96.

Paddison, Mai Halle. "Music and Its Social Mediation: The Concepts of Form and Material in T.V. Adorno's Aesthetics of Music." Thesis, University of Exeter, 1990.

Parker, Everett C. *Religious Television; What to Do and How*. New York: Harper, 1961.

Paul VI (pope). *Sacrosanctum Concilium*. December 4, 1963. www.vatican.va/archive/hist_councils/ii_vatican_council/documents/vat-ii_const_19631204_sacrosanctum-concilium_en.html.

Peck, Janice. *The Gods of Televangelism*. Cresskill, NJ: Hampton, 1993.

Pelinski, Ramón. "Embodiment and Musical Experience." *Trans* 9 (2005). www.sibetrans.com/trans/articulo/178/embodiment-and-musical-experience.

Percy, Martyn. Review of *Towards a Theology of Church Growth*, edited by David Goodhew. *Ecclesiology* 13, no. 1 (January 2017): 136-38.

Peters, Julie Stone. *Theatre of the Book, 1480–1880: Print, Text, and Performance in Europe*. Oxford: University Press, 2000.

Pfaller, Robert. *Interpassivity: The Aesthetics of Delegated Enjoyment*. Edinburgh: Edinburgh University Press, 2017.

Phillips, Peter. "Digital Being." *Crucible*, January 2023. https://crucible.hymnsam.co.uk/articles/2023/january/articles/digital-being/.

Porter, Mark James. *Contemporary Worship Music and Everyday Musical Lives*. Ashgate Congregational Music Studies. London: Routledge, 2017.

Preece, Chloe, Victoria Rodner, and Laryssa Whittaker. "Multiple embodiment relations: sense-making in dissociative experiences." *Consumption Markets & Culture*, 27, no. 2 (2023): 191-215. https://doi.org/10.1080/10253866.2023.2221635.

Przybylski, Liz. *Hybrid Ethnography: Online, Offline, and in Between*. Los Angeles: Sage, 2020.

Rabinow, Paul. *Anthropos Today: Reflections on Modern Equipment*. Princeton, NJ: Princeton University Press, 2009.

Rathey, Markus. "Printing, Politics and 'A Well-Regulated Church Music': A New Perspective on J. S. Bach's Mühlhausen Cantatas." *Early Music* 44, no. 3 (2016): 449-60.

Reyland, Nicholas W., and Rebecca Thumpston, eds. *Music, Analysis, and the Body: Experiments, Explorations, and Embodiments*. Analysis in Context: Leuven Studies in Musicology 6. Leuven: Peeters, 2018.

Rienstra, Debra, Ron Rienstra, Clayton Schmit, and Todd Johnson. *Worship Words: Discipling Language for Faithful Ministry*. Illustrated ed. Grand Rapids, MI: Baker Academic, 2009.

Bibliography

Robb, Hamish. "Imagined, Supplemental Sound in Nineteenth-Century Piano Music: Towards a Fuller Understanding of Musical Embodiment." *Music Theory Online* 21, no. 3 (2015). https://mtosmt.org/issues/mto.15.21.3/mto.15.21.3.robb.html.

Rohde, Marieke, Massimiliano Di Luca, and Marc O. Ernst. "The Rubber Hand Illusion: Feeling of Ownership and Proprioceptive Drift Do Not Go Hand in Hand." *PloS One* 6, no. 6 (2011): e21659.

Ruberg, Bonnie "Bo," and Daniel Lark. "Livestreaming from the Bedroom: Performing Intimacy Through Domestic Space on Twitch." *Convergence* 27, no. 3 (2021): 679-95.

Ruff, Anthony. "After Vatican II: Are We All Protestants Now? Or Are We All Catholics Now?" *The Hymn* 64, no. 1 (Winter 2013): 6-12.

Saliers, Don E. *Music and Theology*. Nashville: Abingdon, 2010.

Santos Boia, Pedro. "Antoine Hennion, The Passion for Music: A Sociology of Mediation: Translated by Margaret Rigaud and Peter Collier, Farnham, Ashgate, 2015, 339 p." *Transposition*, no. 6 (2016). https://doi.org/10.4000/transposition.1473.

Schuler, Richard J. "Reviews: 'Music Printing in Renaissance Venice: The Scotto Press (1529–1572)' by Jane A. Bernstein." *Sacred Music* 126, no. 1 (1999): 26-26.

Sigurdson, Ola. "How to Speak of the Body? Embodiment Between Phenomenology and Theology." *Studia Theologica* 62, no. 1 (2008): 25-43.

Skelchy, Russell P. "The Afterlife of Colonial Radio in Christian Missionary Broadcasting of the Philippines." *South East Asia Research* 28, no. 3 (2020): 344-62.

Smith, Justin E. H. *The Internet Is Not What You Think It Is: A History, a Philosophy, a Warning*. Princeton, NJ: Princeton University Press, 2022.

Steuernagel, Marcell Silva. *Church Music Through the Lens of Performance*. Congregational Music Studies. London: Routledge, 2021.

Taylor, Steve. "Lockdown Ecclesiologies: The Limits and Possibilities of Enforced Online First Expressions." In *Ecclesiology for a Digital Church*, edited by Heidi A. Campbell and John Dyer, 153-72. London: SCM Press, 2021.

Taylor, W. David O. "How to Lead Online Worship Without Losing Your Soul—or Body." *Christianity Today*, March 17, 2020. www.christianitytoday.com/pastors/2020/march-web-exclusives/how-to-lead-online-worship-without-losing-your-soul-or-body.html.

Thompson, Deanna A. "Christ Is Really Present, Even in Holy Communion via Online Worship." *Liturgy* 35, no. 4 (2020): 18-24.

Thornton, Daniel, and Mark Evans. "YouTube: A New Mediator of Christian Community." In *Congregational Music-Making and Community in a Mediated Age*, edited by Anna Nekola and Thomas Wagner, 141-60. Burlington, VT: Ashgate, 2015.

Turino, Thomas. *Music as Social Life: The Politics of Participation*. Chicago Studies in Ethnomusicology. Chicago: University of Chicago Press, 2008.

Uvi. "Ultima Thule Theme 3 'Close in the Distance' (Official Lyrics in Subtitles)—FFXIV OST." February 11, 2022. Video, 10:30. www.youtube.com/watch?v=1aAU1O2mhvs.

Valiquet, Patrick. "A Managed Risk: Mediated Musicianships in a Networked Laptop Orchestra." *Contemporary Music Review* 37, no. 5-6 (2018): 646-65.

Van Opstal, Sandra Maria. *The Next Worship: Glorifying God in a Diverse World*. Downers Grove, IL: InterVarsity Press, 2015.

Vavilova, Zhanna E. "Virtual Satisfaction as a Symptom of Interpassivity in Modern Society." *Society and Security Insights* 4, no. 2 (2021): 132-40.

Venable, Hannah Lyn. "The Weight of Bodily Presence in Art and Liturgy." *Religions* 12, no. 3 (2021): 164.

Vlogbrothers. "Planets Don't Exist." October 7, 2022. Video, 13:59. www.youtube.com/watch?v=S2L0sWMEG-A&t=621s.

Wagner, Rachel. *Godwired: Religion, Ritual, and Virtual Reality*. Media, Religion, and Culture. London: Routledge, 2012.

Wagner, Tom. "Music as Mediated Object, Music as Medium: Towards a Media Ecological View of Congregational Music." In *Congregational Music-Making and Community in a Mediated Age*, edited by Anna Nekola and Thomas Wagner, 25-44. Burlington, VT: Ashgate, 2015.

Ward, Mark. *Air of Salvation: The Story of Christian Broadcasting*. Grand Rapids, MI: Baker Books, 1994.

———. *The Lord's Radio: Gospel Music Broadcasting and the Making of Evangelical Culture, 1920–1960*. Jefferson, NC: McFarland, 2017.

Warren, Tish Harrison. "Why Churches Should Drop Their Online Services." *New York Times*, January 30, 2022. www.nytimes.com/2022/01/30/opinion/church-online-services-covid.html.

Weigel, Taylor. "Online Spaces: Technological, Institutional, and Social Practices That Foster Connections Through Instagram and Twitch." Thesis, Colorado State University, 2020.

Whittaker, Laryssa. "Experiments in real-time hybrid performance: Innovating in the capture of facial expressions for live hybrid performances for the metaverse." Egham, UK: StoryFutures, Royal Holloway, University of London, 2023. https://www.storyfutures.com/uploads/images/resources/MetaMirror-case-study-report-web-version.pdf.

———. "'Onboarding and offboarding in virtual reality: A user-centred framework for audience experience across genres and spaces." *Convergence: International Journal of Research into New Media Technologies*, July 17, 2023. https://doi.org/10.1177/13548565231187329.

Williams, Mike. "FFXIV Streamer Zepla Finds Refuge from Ukrainian Crisis in Poland." Fanbyte, February 24, 2022. www.fanbyte.com/news/ffxiv-streamer-zepla-hq-ukraine-safety-poland/.

Witte, Marleen de. "Modes of Binding, Moments of Bonding. Mediating Divine Touch in Ghanaian Pentecostalism and Traditionalism." In *Aesthetic Formations: Media,*

Religion, and the Senses, edited by Birgit Meyer, 183-205. New York: Palgrave Macmillan, 2009.

Work to Game. "FFXIV FanFest 2021 Was Legendary | Welcome Back Soken." May 17, 2021. Video, 20:04. www.youtube.com/watch?v=RZ8l37z96qw.

Wren, Brian A. *Praying Twice: The Music and Words of Congregational Song*. Louisville, KY: Westminster John Knox, 2000.

Wright, N. T. *Paul and the Faithfulness of God*. Minneapolis: Fortress, 2013.

Yale Youth Ministry Institute. "Dr. Stephanie Paulsell and Vanessa Zoltan on Building Community." July 10, 2018. Video, 4:25. www.youtube.com/watch?v=Z4uirQkGot0.

———. "Dr. Stephanie Paulsell and Vanessa Zoltan on Imagination & Creativity." June 27, 2018. Video, 1:16:41. www.youtube.com/watch?v=0I755tJlakc.

———. "Dr. Stephanie Paulsell and Ms. Vanessa Zoltan on Ritual and Millennials." July 10, 2018. Video, 2:56. www.youtube.com/watch?v=q2TFIb9n6k4.

Young, Gray, ed. *The Internet*. The Reference Shelf 70. New York: H. W. Wilson, 1998.

Zepla HQ. "I've Left Ukraine—a Personal Update." March 18, 2022. Video, 15:43. www.youtube.com/watch?v=ilwDDRYBI0g.

ZepLIVE. "Zepla Playthrough of Endwalker MSQ—The Final Day (Timestamps Inside)." December 28, 2021. Video, 5:38:11. www.youtube.com/watch?v=JhzyzPCRwng.

———. "Zepla Updates on Her Home in Ukraine." April 20, 2022. Video, 15:54. www.youtube.com/watch?v=fZRV6tHERNk.

———. "Zepla's Heatbreaking Story of Escaping Ukraine." March 2, 2022. Video, 31:36. www.youtube.com/watch?v=2yxLfagXli0.

Index

active participation, 17-18, 48-50, 53, 60, 75, 150-51
affordance, 2, 98, 120-22, 124, 141-42, 153-54
assemblage, 82-86
attention economy, 17, 23, 25, 28-31, 32-35, 43-45, 102, 145, 149
Berger, Teresa, 13, 74-75, 80-81, 88
body schema, 64-66, 70, 99, 128-29, 151
Burton-Edwards, Taylor, 9, 38-40
Campbell, Heidi A., 9, 35-37, 40-42, 89-90, 93-95, 108, 112-13, 121, 124, 135-36
church music, 17, 19-20, 24, 35, 42-43, 45, 59, 101, 105, 109-10, 149
    church music studies, 7, 125, 150, 155
    purposes of, 114-18, 124
    using various technologies, 106, 144, 154-55
community building online, 123-24, 125-33, 133-37, 137-40
Covid-19, churches' responses to, 1-2, 20-21, 23, 35-37, 43, 112-13
criteria for evaluating online communal practices, 119-21
dichotomies, 7, 17-19, 46-47, 50, 95, 107, 109, 113-14, 150-53
digital ethnography, 2, 6, 8-9, 20
digital revolution, 5, 12, 97, 109, 154
    See also Internet, as a technological revolution
embodiment, 5, 17-19, 46, 61-63, 73-75, 113, 120, 140, 147, 150-53
    and inclusion, 5, 18, 68-73, 75-76, 151-52
    and music, 5, 63-65, 66-68
    and online technologies, 5, 69-73, 96-100, 128-29
hybridity, 19-20, 109-14
    hybrid ministry, 2-3, 6-7, 19-20, 111-13, 123, 153

I-Thou stance, 17, 31-34, 43, 45, 149
Internet, as a technological revolution, 23-24, 26-28, 29-30, 35-36, 43, 45, 47, 75, 80, 86-87, 97, 107-9, 114, 149, 154
interpassivity, 3, 18, 50-53, 55-60, 113, 120, 129-30, 150-51, 158
invisible technologies, 27, 65, 68, 79-80, 82, 89-90, 92, 149
Iovino, Joe, 10, 38
media ecologies, 12-17, 37, 84
mediation, 14, 18-19, 37, 58, 75, 77-92, 152
    in/as music, 82-86
    philosophy of, 86-89, 91
    in relationship to God, 80, 89-92
    vanishing mediators, 78-80, 88, 91.
        See invisible technologies
    worship as mediated/unmediated, 78-82, 92
Nekola, Anna, 13-14, 125
Norton, Allison, 10, 38-39, 72
online communities, 2, 5, 7-9, 12, 16, 20, 23-24, 42, 71-72, 92-93, 123-4, 125-32, 133-37, 137-40, 140-42, 144-45, 147, 153-54
Phillips, Peter, 10, 73-74, 81, 90-91, 141-44, 146
Soto, DJ, 11, 42-43, 69-72, 102-3, 105-7, 146-47
transformative moral commitment, 17, 31, 33, 43-45, 102, 149
virtuality, 2, 7, 17, 19, 47, 61, 77, 90, 92-108, 109, 147, 150, 152-53
    shifting terminology in scholarship, 93-96
    virtual environments, 69-71, 97-98, 103, 106, 111, 152
    virtual fieldwork (*see* digital ethnography)
    virtual reality, 11, 42-43, 69, 80, 96-102, 102-7, 152
    virtual reality and music, 104-6
    virtual reality as pro-social, 98-102, 103-4
Whittaker, Laryssa, 11, 102-5